Hijinx

Hijinx

Edited by Val Hill

PARTHIAN

Parthian
The Old Surgery
Napier Street
Cardigan
SA43 1ED

www.parthianbooks.co.uk

First published in 2006
© The Authors 2006
All Rights Reserved

ISBN 1-902638-77-8
   9 781902 638775

Cover design by Marc Jennings
Inner design by type@lloydrobson.com
Printed and bound by Dinefwr Press, Llandybïe, Wales

Published with the financial support of the Welsh
Books Council

British Library Cataloguing in Publication Data
A cataloguing record for this book is available from the
British Library

Contents

Introduction

I am delighted Parthian are publishing this volume of three plays produced by Hijinx Theatre. Since 1990, Hijinx have commissioned a total of twenty plays, some of which – like the ones in this book – are for community audiences, and some for adults with learning disabilities. As with much new work produced by small companies who perform in non traditional venues, once the tour is over the play disappears, remaining only in the memory of those who saw it. There is a huge canon of work produced in Wales over the last twenty to thirty years, much of it has disappeared, and so to see plays in print, leaving a legacy for others, is a great joy.

Hijinx was born in 1981 and has its roots in improvisation and experimentation. In the early years the company devised work, often with the help of a writer – usually Charles Way. As the theatre making process evolved and the ensemble of actors moved to pastures new, the desire to tell stories which would both challenge and delight our audiences lead to a new era of commissioning plays on a regular basis. Throughout our journey, from devising to commissioning, our audiences remain at the heart of our work.

The three plays in this book are all very different, although in each case they are the first plays written for Hijinx, by these writers.

Greg Cullen's *Paul Robeson Knew My Father* is an epic tale of a small boy's quest; his search for answers in a world in which he feels out-of-joint. The giant figure of Paul Robeson, actor, movie hero and man with a velvet voice, looms like a colossus in his consciousness, inspiring him and always offering hope. Greg himself grew up in an Irish community in north London, in the 1950s, seeing

1

Proud Valley was for him a life-changing experience. In his directors notes he describes Robeson as, 'Huge but gentle, strong but vulnerable, clear but compassionate... I had met my hero. I wanted him to look after me.' The roots of *Paul Robeson Knew My Father* can be traced to that day.

The play deals with many social issues, like single motherhood in the south Wales valleys in the late 1950s and racism, at a time when you were a stranger if you came from another valley. The action is set against the backdrop of Welsh history, particularly the tremendous bond formed between Robeson and the South Wales Miners. When we hear the original transatlantic telephone conversation between Will Paynter of the SW Miners Federation and Robeson, the hairs on my neck still stand on end – I am there in Porthcawl Pavilion in 1957. To sit beside Tyrone O'Sullivan at a performance in the Pavilion during the 1999 Miners' Eisteddfod and hear him quietly singing along is a memory burnt deep in the psyche. Such was the response when we first toured the play in 1999 that we re-toured it immediately to larger venues in the spring of 2000 – an unheard of first for Hijinx – and undertook a new production in 2004.

Dreaming Amelia was Sharon Morgan's first full length play. Like *Paul Robeson Knew My Father*, it is inspired by an iconic figure – Amelia Earhart – and her transatlantic flight of 1928 which landed in Burry Port. Sharon grew up in Carmarthenshire not far from Burry Port and yet knew nothing about Amelia's flight until much later. As a feminist, this added to her awareness that major achievements by women are often hidden from history.

It is a play about artistic integrity as a metaphor for personal integrity, based on the belief that by discovering our true selves we can enrich the lives of others. It faces the dilemma as to whether an exploration of the self can only be at the cost of the happiness of others, and poses the question as to whether it is possible to follow your dream while also inspiring others to follow theirs. It is a tremendously lyrical play with a strong dance element that weaves flowing words with flowing movement and creates a work of great beauty and gritty meaning. It is a play about self-discovery and taking risks in the search for your inner self. We toured it in the autumn of 2002 with a positive response from audiences, although Sharon's interpretation of Martha Graham caused some controversy in the dance world.

Both *Paul Robeson Knew My Father* and *Dreaming Amelia* are plays inspired by real people and tell stories of how ordinary people can achieve extraordinary things when they follow their dreams with courage and determination.

Lewis Davies's *Spinning The Round Table* takes us on a very different journey. It is a play about public perception, media spin and political ambition, with a glimpse of what this does to the lives of people who live entirely in the public spotlight. While it does take the love triangle from the Arthurian legend, by placing it in the cut-throat world of twenty-first century politics it takes us a million miles away from the Hollywood version of Camelot. Yet, behind the spotlight, universal human emotions of love, desire, ambition and friendship are juggled with public perception. Arthur's idealistic dream of creating a better world battles with the overwhelming tide of media manip- ulation, driving his personal life dangerously close to destruction.

As I write this, in August 2005, we have not yet started rehearsing the play, so for me the power of the words are still on the page. I look forward to seeing it on the stage and responding to it as a real experience, adding to the kaleidoscope of words and images that swirl around my brain.

We have worked with many writers over the last fifteen years, all of whom have woven tales of magic for audiences in small communities throughout the length and breadth of Wales and England, but I feel the need to give a

3

special mention to Charles Way and Larry Allan who have contributed hugely to our growth and development. They have very contrasting styles but both have the ability to take us on that magic carpet to another place, while remaining firmly rooted in universal themes and human emotions. Along with all the writers who have written for us, they have made us laugh, made us cry and made us ask questions.

Finally, I would like to thank all the touring and production teams whose brilliance and skill have made the stories come alive, particularly the touring teams whose resilience and good humour can be worn somewhat thin on a cold, rainy, November night as they load the van before another drive to another town, where they will, once again, transform a village hall and transport the audience to another place. They have all embraced the belief in the power of theatre to transform and inspire people in their daily lives.

As we move towards our twenty-fifth birthday, in 2006, I am confident that we will be commissioning many more plays, and I continue to nurture the dream that one day we can ask a writer to write for more than four actors.

Val Hill
Administrative Director
Hijinx Theatre

Val Hill and Lewis Davies

Paul Robeson
knew My Father
PG
by Greg Cullen

HIJINX
THEATRE

Paul Robeson Knew My Father

Greg Cullen

Paul Robeson Knew My Father was commissioned by Hijinx Theatre with the support of an ACW grant. It toured in the autumn of 1999, with a First Performance on Tuesday 28th September 1999 at the Drama Studio, Whitchurch High School, Cardiff.

Cast:

Gethyn	–	Mark Howell East
Sandra	–	Melissa Vincent
Ron	–	Gareth Potter
George Cumberbatch	–	Declan Wilson

Creative Team:

Director	–	Greg Cullen
Musical Director	–	Paula Gardiner
Designer	–	Claire Leadbeater
Choreographer	–	Pebs Jones
Production Manager	–	Ian Hill
Stage Manager	–	Cath Husband
Lighting Designers	–	Cath Husband
		Ian Hill

For my parents, Patricia and Stanley Cullen
with whom, as a very small boy, I first fell in love
with Paul Robeson.
Greg Cullen

Act One

Projection: Paul Robeson, in the opening shots of 'Proud Valley'.

GETHYN, a man of fifty-two, enters the light. Robeson sings.

ROBESON: Sometimes I feel like a motherless child,
Sometimes I feel like a motherless child,
Sometimes I feel like a motherless child,
A long ways from home,
A long ways from home.
Come my brother, a longs ways from home,
A long ways from home.

The film freezes on Robeson, smiling.

GETHYN (*as boy*): There he was, holes in his boots, smile like a moon hanging in the sky, Paul Robeson, my Dada's butty! 'Will he come back and sing for us?' 'One day' my mother would say, 'one day'. It was always 'one day' back in the fifties. Now it's... now.

Film stops. Stage lights up on GETHYN. His mother, SANDRA, sits in 1956, aged twenty-eight. She is listening to the radio.

GETHYN: Sunday mornings, one ear on the radio, the other on the hiss of fat hitting the side of the oven. My stomach ached, my legs grew weak, trembling from the torture of a terrace filling with the promise of roasties and mint. 'It's the Billy Cotton Band show!' I hated that, but 'Two Way Family Favourites', ah now then...

'This request is for Corporal Ken Hughes in BFPO 49, from his loving wife Liz, who hopes he's wearing the vest she knitted for Christmas.' Then on he came...

Robeson sings 'Old Man River'. GETHYN speaks as he did when he was nine years old.

GETHYN (*as boy*): It's him.

SANDRA: Hush, now.

GETHYN: No one sounded like him, no one could. God only gave that voice to one man, and he gave it to him for a reason.

GETHYN (*as boy*): Did my Da sing this one with him?

SANDRA: Maybe.

GETHYN (*as boy*): Did he?

SANDRA: It's possible.

GETHYN (*as boy*): Did he though?

SANDRA: Yes.

GETHYN (*as boy*): What was it like?

SANDRA: Like now.

GETHYN (*as boy*): The deep resonance filtered through the plaster, reverberated in the bricks and flowed along the grain of timbers. In that voice was an unassailable dignity that caused one's back to straighten, one's head to lift and look forward; something in that voice gave me a sense of self respect. Although I was barely aware of how much I needed it.

The song ends. They look at each other and sing. GETHYN is a boy again.

BOTH: 'They can't stop us singing.'

They laugh.

GETHYN (*as boy*): Was Paul Robeson really that big?

SANDRA: Huge.

GETHYN (*as boy*): As big as the door.

SANDRA: Bigger, he'd never have got in here.

GETHYN (*as boy*): No...

SANDRA: He'd have had to stand out in the street and sing in through the window... even then he might have banged his head on the sky.

GETHYN (*as boy*): I bet my Dad was nearly as tall.

SANDRA (*laughing*): No, not exactly.

GETHYN (*as boy*): Why not?

SANDRA: Why not? I don't know.

GETHYN (*as boy*): I bet he was bigger than most round here.

SANDRA: He was big enough for coal.

GETHYN (*as boy*): That's big isn't it?

SANDRA: Big enough so's not to keep banging his head.

GETHYN (*as boy*): I bet when Paul Robeson was a miner he kept banging his head.

SANDRA: That was only a film.

GETHYN (*as boy*): Dad probably looked after him, told him when to duck.

SANDRA: Probably.

GETHYN (*as boy*): Did you love him?

SANDRA: Paul Robeson?

GETHYN (*as boy*): No, my Dad.

SANDRA: Why do you ask?

GETHYN (*as boy*): I don't know.

GETHYN: Mam worked to keep me, assembling, factory work it was. Nimble fingers see, made for the piano, but they had to find other uses. One holiday, to keep me out of trouble she gave me pocket money to go see 'Proud Valley' starring Paul Robeson, which was showing at the local flea pit. I went every day for a week. After every matinee I hid under the seat and waited for the next showing. I knew see, that my Da had once sung with Paul Robeson.

Projection: 'The Proud Valley'. The miners march through town, on their way to London.

GETHYN: Perhaps, I got to thinking, my Da was one of these men? (*Acts along to the film, imagining he is with Robeson, marching to London.*)

AN ACTOR (*calling from off-stage*): Get out the way of the screen you daft bugger!

GETHYN (*as boy*): Sorry.

Film ends.

GETHYN: The only other thing I knew for certain was that Da had been killed during the war. Never laid eyes on me, or me upon him. I didn't have no relatives nearby. We'd moved valley before I was born. I had a grandmother. I'd seen her once, black coat and a growl set into her face so deep that even when she smiled the jowls flapped and dragged any joy from her eyes. God she were ugly and to be honest I didn't mind not seeing her too often. The only man that came by was 'uncle' Ron.

RON, aged thirty-five, enters wearing a white fifties' motorbike helmet and carrying an abundant cabbage, which he proudly presents to SANDRA.

RON: Got you a cabbage.

SANDRA: Ta.

RON: I haven't got long.

They look at GETHYN.

RON: Boy all right?

13

SANDRA: Fine? You're all right aren't you Geth? Teacher played a Paul Robeson song at assembly, didn't she?

GETHYN nods.

RON: Your Mam was asking after you?

SANDRA: Oh, yes?

RON: Her heart's bad again.

SANDRA: Is it?

RON: Could be it this time. They've had the doctor round. You should go see her.

SANDRA: She knows where the bus stop is.

RON: She can't die on the number forty nine.

SANDRA: That woman died years ago.

RON: Have it your way. It's a good cabbage that, comes from Gordon, grew it on his allotment, like. (*He moves close to SANDRA.*) Haven't got long , isn't it? Told the Missus I only be an hour.

SANDRA: Gethyn, go on up to your room, love, read a book or something, there's a good boy.

The imaginary Gethyn goes.

RON: What's the matter with him?

SANDRA: D'you want a cuppa?

RON: Got any coffee?

SANDRA: I only got Camp.

RON: What happened to the coffee I bought you?

SANDRA: I drank it. (*She turns the radio on.*)

RON: Oh, great!

SANDRA: Isn't that what I was supposed to do with it?

Paul Robeson sings 'Lazin'.

RON: Wanted you today. Saw you going off to the lavvy. (*He puts his arms around SANDRA.*) Would have come in only Fran-bloody-Roberts walked by.

SANDRA: Don't swear in my house.

RON starts kissing her SANDRA's neck.

RON: Took your time didn't you?

SANDRA: I needed a fag.

RON: The others talk; say, 'How come I never threaten you with your cards?'

SANDRA starts dancing with RON. She flirts.

SANDRA: That's my privilege isn't it?

RON: Privilege is it?

SANDRA: Don't kid yourself.

RON: Not sure I am. You always come back for more.

SANDRA: It's Gordon's cabbages, not sure I can live without them.

They enjoy the dance.

Lights down. Lights up on GETHYN.

GETHYN: Down the road, on the new estate, lived Big Glyn. He'd once been Lodge Chairman. When he retired they bought him a record player and two records – Mario Lanza and Paul Robeson.

Robeson sings 'Joe Hill'.

GETHYN: Glyn couldn't sing no more on account of his lungs, like, and that music frustrated the hell out of him, but he liked to let me listen. Don't know why. Perhaps he knew more about me than I did. Or perhaps, as I thought then, he took a shine to me because my Da and Paul were best Butties. When 'uncle' Ron came to visit I took to skiving off to Big Glyn's, he'd sit spitting dust into a bucket, a black cesspit full of demons, and wheezing along to the music.

I'd picture my Da, the war hero, landing on the beaches of Normandy, or a Desert Rat in the tank turret alongside Monty. Submarine commander, spitfire pilot, jungle fighter or tail-gun-charlie, which?

Light up on SANDRA in another time and place.

SANDRA: For goodness sake, what does it matter? He was in the war, that's all.

16

GETHYN: Everywhere... across the world fighting fascists. Paul Robeson and my Da, they hated fascists.

SANDRA: There's nothing else to know! (*She is tearful.*)

GETHYN: Because he was a spy I bet, on a top secret mission! But it was all right, 'cause I knew, I knew that one day Paul Robeson would come back to Wales and he'll tell me all about my Da.

Sounds of a train pulling out of a station. Lights up on GEORGE CUMBERBATCH, who enters wearing a raincoat and hat, carrying a cricket bat and a small suitcase. He pulls up his collar against the cold. GETHYN watches him in amazement. GEORGE freezes. Lights up on SANDRA.

SANDRA: You can't have seen Paul Robeson.

GETHYN (*as boy*): I'm telling you. He was sneaking down the road so's nobody would notice he was back. Probably wants to get settled in first. He's going to surprise everyone. I bet he's down the pub tonight. He'll sing to us walking down the road. We'll all come out of our houses and cheer and everything. Carry him on our shoulders... if he isn't too heavy, like. It was him I'm telling you.

SANDRA: It can't have been him.

GETHYN (*as boy*): How d'you know?

SANDRA: Because Paul Robeson isn't allowed out of America, they took his passport away.

GETHYN (*as boy*): Who did?

SANDRA: The President.

GETHYN (*as boy*): What for?

SANDRA: For saying something bad about it.

GETHYN (*as boy*): But America's on our side.

SANDRA: They don't treat coloured people very well.

GETHYN (*as boy*): What like Negroes?

SANDRA: Yes, Negroes. And he can't leave America without a passport. He's like a prisoner.

GETHYN (*as boy*): That's it! It was Paul Robeson!

SANDRA: How d'you work that out?

GETHYN (*as boy*): That's how come he was trying not to be noticed, 'cause he's on the run from America, like. He's sneaked out to Wales.

SANDRA: He's just someone up from Tiger Bay.

GETHYN (*as boy*): No, I know Paul Robeson when I see him.

SANDRA: Was he very tall?

GETHYN (*as boy*): His head was touching the clouds.

SANDRA: Maybe it was then. (*She smiles to herself.*)

GEORGE is unpacking his case. Young GETHYN pushes a note, as if under the door.

GEORGE *(reading the note):* 'Don't worry Paul, your secret's safe with me.' *(He is nonplussed.)*

GETHYN: I knew, see, he'd come back to Wales 'cause he missed my Dada. He'd sung at his funeral I'll bet.

Projection: A scene from 'The Proud Valley' where Robeson sings at the eistedfford, in honour of Dick Parry. As Robeson speaks, GETHYN recites the words.

GETHYN *(as Robeson):* I didn't know Dick Parry for long, but I lived and worked with him enough to realise that he was a man, every inch of him. Sometimes when we were alone I used to sing him this song, which we're now going to sing for you.

The film sound is restored, as the choir sing 'Deep River My Home is Over Jordan'.

GETHYN *(as boy):* The valley wept when my Dad died, that's why no one can bring themselves to talk about it. He was a great man, my Da, everyone loved him. I bet he and Mam had put Paul up in our house when he first arrived, penniless, holes in his shoes, straight off a boat from Cardiff. Now he was back, back to look after us.

A recording of Robeson singing, 'My Curly Headed Baby'. GEORGE becomes Robeson in GETHYN's imagination, miming to the recording. He dances with a jacket, as if it is a child, cuddling it in his arms. Lights fade. SANDRA enters.

SANDRA: Where've you been?

GETHYN *(as boy):* Up Paul's house.

SANDRA: Jones?

GETHYN (*as boy*): No, Robeson.

SANDRA: You're not bothering that man are you?

GETHYN (*as boy*): No! Just watching him.

SANDRA: Watching him?

GETHYN (*as boy*): Through his curtains.

SANDRA: Gethyn, you can't do that! It's spying.

GETHYN (*as boy*): Like Da!

SANDRA: What?

GETHYN (*as boy*): Da was a spy.

SANDRA: He was not! Look Geth, your Da was not a spy and that man isn't, can't be, Paul Robeson. His name is George something. Honestly, you'll be called a peeping Tom. He's not even American. He's working for the council on the roads. Geth, listen. Geth? Gethyn, come back!

GETHYN: I knew better. Us kids knew better. They'd run up and touch him for luck, black men's lucky, see? And Paul Robeson, well, he must ha' been the luckiest of the lot. Course, you don't hang around after, like. Just get your luck and scarper. But me, I was going to stay, it was all right for me, 'cause Paul Robeson knew my father.

GEORGE (*practising his strokes with a cricket bat, imagining himself to be in a test match. He commentates in a posh, English accent*): Benows bowls to Sobers. Oh my word, he's lashed it! (*He circles his hips, as in Sobers' celebration routine.*) And... oh dear, this is the sort of thing that gets the West Indies a bad name. (*He laughs.*)

GETHYN sings outside the room. GEORGE is a little frightened, then becomes enraged.

GETHYN (*as boy*): Ole man river, that old man river
                    He must know something
                    But don't say nothing,
                    He just keeps rolling, he keeps on rolling
                                                        along...

GEORGE: What you want? Eh? Just clear off and leave me alone, you hear?

GETHYN (*as boy*): 'He don't plant taters
                    He don't plant cotton
                    And them that plants 'em is soon
                                                forgotten...'

GEORGE: What's the matter with you people?

GEORGE runs out and shouts at GETHYN, waving the cricket bat like a weapon.

GEORGE: I said get lost!

The imaginary Gethyn runs away, upset. GEORGE is shocked to find it was just a child.

RON is at the house. GETHYN sits.

21

RON: What's the matter with him now?

SANDRA: He's upset.

RON: I can see that.

SANDRA (*to GETHYN*): He put his faith is someone when all around him were warning him not too, isn't that right? Best learn young, Geth, don't want to be daft all your life.

RON: Takes after his Dada does he?

SANDRA: What?

RON: Must take after his Da?

Deathly silence.

RON: It was a compliment.

SANDRA: A compliment?

RON: I'm saying, you ain't stupid, so it must be his father.

GETHYN (*as boy*): Don't you come into my Da's house an' call him stupid. He was brainy, more brains than you, everyone said so, everyone loved him, not like you, everyone hates you 'cause you're a scab.

RON: Who said I was?

GETHYN runs to his bedroom.

RON: Oi! You little bastard.

SANDRA: Get out.

RON: Sorry.

SANDRA: Get out. I told you, don't you ever swear in my house.

RON: All right, I said I'm sorry.

SANDRA: Get out.

RON: I can't go back yet, I told her I was working late.

SANDRA: Leave.

RON: Come on, don't be like this.

SANDRA does not relent.

RON: I brought you a pound of sprouts. Right then, see you at work. (*He makes to leave.*) Hey, while we're at it, you watch yourself tomorrow, getting a bit too cocky for my liking. (*He exits.*)

SANDRA calms herself down, then goes to see GETHYN.

GETHYN (*as boy*): I hate him.

SANDRA: He didn't mean it.

GETHYN (*as boy*): Why does he have to come round here?

SANDRA: Just gives me a lift home that's all.

GETHYN (*as boy*): He's always here.

SANDRA: He's a friend.

GETHYN (*as boy*): I ain't calling him 'uncle' no more.

SANDRA: Gethyn.

GETHYN (*as boy*): Why doesn't he go and see his own wife.

SANDRA: Gethyn that's enough.

GETHYN (*as boy*): Why don't you tell his wife to look after him!

SANDRA: That's enough! His wife isn't well. Look this is my business, you understand? Not yours, not anybody else's. And God help you if you ever mention it outside!

SANDRA slaps his face. GETHYN pulls away from her, resentfully. SANDRA regrets her actions. GEORGE knocks at their door.

SANDRA: He's back. Probably wants his sprouts. Now you stay here. (*She opens the door.*) Oh.

GEORGE: Erm, I er... wanted to say sorry... to your son. I think it is your son. He's been up at...

SANDRA: Don't apologise...

GEORGE: I think I scared him. You see I've had people...

SANDRA: It's my fault...

GEORGE: Well, I thought perhaps he was...

SANDRA: I tried telling him...

GEORGE: some other guys...

SANDRA: But he wouldn't have it, see?

GEORGE: I was a little fierce.

SANDRA: He thinks you're Paul Robeson.

GEORGE: Who?

SANDRA: Paul Robeson.

GEORGE: Right. Is he local?

SANDRA: Paul Robeson? Lord no, he's famous, world famous, he's a singer.

GEORGE: A singer?! Your son wouldn't want to hear me sing, not even on a Sunday!

SANDRA: Perhaps you could do us both a favour and tell him yourself.

GEORGE: Well, is Mr..?

SANDRA: Williams, no he's not.

GEORGE: Another time perhaps...

SANDRA: We lost him in the war.

GEORGE: I'm sorry.

GETHYN (*as boy*): You know that, he sang with you.

They turn to see GETHYN. The imaginary Gethyn pushes past them.

SANDRA: Gethyn! You can't keep running away.

GEORGE: I'll go see if I can talk it out of him. Good day to you Mrs Williams. Sorry if I've caused any...

SANDRA: No, no, you haven't, honestly, it's just 'us' I'm afraid. (*She goes into her house. We see her stress.*)

Lights down. GEORGE approaches GETHYN. An exterior.

GEORGE: Forgive me for waving my bat at you? (*He waits, then states very deliberately:*) my name is George Cumberbatch.

GETHYN (*as boy*): You just made that up!

GEORGE: No I didn't.

GETHYN (*as boy*): Cumberbatch? I'm not stupid.

GEORGE: Look kid, I'm not this Paul Robeson.

GETHYN (*as boy*): He's a Negro.

GEORGE: Aren't we all?

GETHYN (*as boy*): Was that a joke?

GEORGE: Kind of.

GETHYN (*as boy*): Let's hear you sing. He's got the best voice in the world. He hardly has to move a muscle and this sound comes out that makes the walls hum. You speak American.

GEORGE: No, I come from British Guyana.

GETHYN (*as boy*): There's no such place, you're making this up! Paul Robeson comes to Wales. He made a film. He sacrifices his life for us. They sang together, him and Da. Then Da got shot down over France.

GEORGE: Really?

GETHYN (*as boy*): He was being parachuted behind enemy lines. His mission was to destroy the Doodlebugs. Did you fight?

GEORGE: Merchant navy.

GETHYN (*as boy*): A Gunner?

GEORGE: Purser's clerk.

GETHYN (*as boy*): Don't believe you. You're tall. Paul Robeson was a giant. Played American football.

GEORGE: Is that right?

GETHYN (*as boy*): And he was a lawyer.

GEORGE: A lawyer.

GETHYN (*as boy*): And he was an actor.

GEORGE: An actor too?

GETHYN (*as boy*): And he was Othello.

GEORGE: What's that?

GETHYN (*as boy*): And a poet.

GEORGE: Anything else? Could he do magic?

GEORGE shows him a disappearing coin trick. GETHYN tries not to be impressed.

GETHYN (*as boy*): No, but my Da could do that, he could make whole people disappear.

GEORGE: Shame I arrived too late to meet these 'remarkable men'.

GETHYN (*as boy*): Big Glyn's got all his records. Big Glyn reckons Robeson's not a communist, 'cause he's a Christian, so what are you, a communist or a socialist?

GEORGE: I don't take any interest in politics.

GETHYN (*as boy*): How come?

GEORGE: I don't want trouble, that's why. I just keep myself to myself. If other people want to fight about this and about that, then let them. I want no part of it.

GETHYN (*as boy*): Sing.

GEORGE: What?

GETHYN (*as boy*): Sing.

GEORGE: I told you, I don't sing.

GETHYN (*as boy*): Sing something, anything.

GEORGE: I don't know anything.

GETHYN (*as boy*): Everyone knows something.

GEORGE: I don't.

GETHYN (*as boy*): You must know a nursery rhyme.

GEORGE: Well, sure, but...

GETHYN (*as boy*): Sing that.

GEORGE: I can't.

GETHYN (*as boy*): Course you can.

GEORGE: 'Brown girl in the ring'.

GETHYN (*as boy*): What's that?

GEORGE: A song! I thought that's what you wanted?!

GETHYN (*as boy*): It is.

GEORGE: Well then!

GETHYN (*as boy*): So sing it.

GEORGE: I am singing it! Give me a chance!

GETHYN (*as boy*): Go on then.

GEORGE (*self-consciously, voice strangled in his throat*): Brown girl in the ring, tra-la-la-la-lee, Brown girl in the ring tra-la-la...'

GETHYN: No, you're not Paul Robeson.

GEORGE shrugs and exits. Lights change to interior.

SANDRA: So let me get this straight: he's not American, he can't sing a note, and he's never even heard of Paul Robeson. Maybe he's a socialist?

GETHYN's disappointment gives her the answer.

SANDRA: Oh well.

Robeson sings 'Go Down Moses'.

GETHYN: The summer wore on and Big Glyn spat his last globule of blackened mucus into his bucket. His wife, Mrs Big Glyn, send a cart round, on it was Glyn's record player and his two records, Mario Lanza and Paul Robeson. Couldn't escape to Big Glyn's no more, so I turned it up as loud as I could to blare out the sound of 'uncle' Ron.

In dance, RON ravishes SANDRA, who grows ever more resentful of his attentions. RON exits.

GEORGE CUMBERBATCH is nervous – people are watching him in the street. He carries a record in a bag. He waits before approaching the Williams' door. SANDRA opens it.

SANDRA: Oh, hello.

GEORGE: Good day to you, it's a fine afternoon. I wondered if I might have a word with Gethyn?

SANDRA: I'll fetch him now. Everything all right?

GEORGE: Yes.

SANDRA: He hasn't been...?

GEORGE: No, no.

SANDRA: Gethyn! Turn that music down! (*To GEORGE:*) Honestly! It's Mr..?

GEORGE: Cumberbatch.

SANDRA: Sorry?

GEORGE: Cumberbatch.

SANDRA (*shouts to GETHYN*): Mr Cumberpatch!

GEORGE: Batch.

SANDRA doesn't understand.

GEORGE: Cumber*batch*. (*Slightly indignant:*) Where I come from it's a very popular name.

GETHYN arrives.

GEORGE: I got another apology to make to you. When you told me that Paul Robeson was all them things I thought, 'The boy's making it up'. Anyhow, I was in the library and what do I find? A book by Paul Robeson. And

31

what does this book tell me? That everything you said was true. It got me thinking. So I got the train to Cardiff this morning and I bought you this, seeing's how your Daddy sung with him.

GEORGE hands the record to GETHYN.

SANDRA: Well, what do you say? He doesn't get a lot of presents?

GEORGE: Well, you enjoy it.

SANDRA: Well... don't you want to hear it?

GEORGE: I heard a little in the shop.

SANDRA: Do you like coffee?

GEORGE: I do.

SANDRA: I've got some tucked away?

GEORGE hesitates.

SANDRA: I won't bite you.

GEORGE: It's not that.

GEORGE indicates a neighbour is watching. SANDRA sees them too.

SANDRA (*defiantly*): Gethyn put the record on for Mr Cumberbatch.

GEORGE enters the house.

Projection: A scene from 'The Proud Valley', where Robeson is brought home by Dick Parry.

ROBESON: I just want to thank you for the cup of tea and the bite to eat, 'cause I'm going along now.

MRS PARRY: Indeed, I'm not going to let you go at this time of night! We'll find somewhere for you to sleep.

DICK PARRY: He can sleep on the sofa in the front room, can't he?

MRS PARRY: Yes, to be sure.

PHYLLIS: Here, here, didn't I tell you she'd be all right?

ROBESON: Yes.

MRS PARRY: Phyllis, get up those stairs to bed.

MR PARRY: Ah, no Mam, let her stay. I do wish you'd been down there to hear him tonight, a bottom bass like an organ.

Film ends.

Some time later, in the Williams' household:

GEORGE: Every summer my father would take my brother, my sister and me up river. Can't walk far in Guyana before getting in a boat. We'd take the ferry from Georgetown, leave at eight thirty get to Bartica about three in the afternoon. From there we could only travel by canoe...

GETHYN (*as boy*): Canoe?

GEORGE: Dug out canoes – the Indians make them.

GETHYN (*as boy*): Indians?

GEORGE: That's right. They lived there long before the British arrived. It gets confusing see, 'cause the British brought over Indians from India 'cause they knew how to plant rice. So we got Indians an' Indians if you see what I mean? Then come the Chinese too. Negro people like us came from Barbados mostly, 'cause we knew how to grow sugar cane.

SANDRA: What you all live together like?

GEORGE: Pretty much.

SANDRA: Can you vote?

GEORGE: It's coming. Lot of trouble it's causing too.

GETHYN (*as boy*): Did you have your own paddle?

GEORGE: My own paddle?

GETHYN (*as boy*): In the canoe?

GEORGE: We had to! It would take us three days to get up the Essequibo River!

SANDRA: Where did you sleep?

GEORGE: In villages along the way. But you should see the Essequibo river, man I'd be scared of falling in! Where I come from the Caribbean is like glass, can see what going on, but the Essequibo was black. Alligators and all sorts lurking down there and I can't swim. But it was worth it. Sometimes the river was wide and could see the sky, other times it narrowed and the trees arched over our heads. Monkeys looking down on us like we were from another planet. Toucans, parrots, birds of such colour made your eyes sing. And then after three days you'd start to hear this rumbling sound, could feel it in your bones, water started coming at you fast, had to paddle like hell I'm telling you, then we'd hit this bend in the river and there they were – the Kaiteur Falls! The highest waterfall in the whole world, Man. Drops eight hundred feet straight down. It was like travelling along an artery till you find your way to what makes the heart beat.

GETHYN: He may not have been Paul Robeson, but my head was swimming – up the Essequibo river with my own paddle, alligators to the right of me, monkeys up above, me an my Da. Later, I'd sit by the Rhondda, black from coal and hear the parrots squawking.

GEORGE (*reading an LP cover*):   Listen to this: because they won't let Robeson out of the US, right? He stood one foot inside the American border, yeah, and the audience – forty thousand of them – sat on the Canadian side of the border, that way the police couldn't stop it!

SANDRA: No!

GEORGE: It's got his speech here. You'll like this bit Gethyn, 'I just couldn't receive an invitation that could mean more, it is to appear at the Eisteddfod in October, an Eisteddfod given by the miners and by the workers of Wales. Wales, you know, is where I first understood the struggle of White and Negro together. And I hope to be able to get there to do that.'

GETHYN (*as boy*): He's coming! He's coming back to Wales.

SANDRA: When was this?

GEORGE: August 16, 1953.

SANDRA: Four years ago.

GETHYN (*as boy*): Why didn't he come?

SANDRA: They still won't let him out of his country.

GEORGE: Well, I heard that Will Paynter invited him again this year. Maybe they'll let him come this time eh, Gethyn?

GETHYN (*as boy*): Will he still recognise you Mam?

GEORGE: You know him? Well I had no idea I was mixing in such distinguished social circles. When was this?

SANDRA: My husband sang with him once, that's all.

GETHYN (*as boy*): And you met him?

SANDRA: It's got 'Scandaliz' My Name' on it too, Geth! That's one of our favourites isn't it?

SANDRA begins to sing, animating the song. GETHYN joins in.

SANDRA: I met my sister the other day,
             I gave her my right hand,
             And just as soon as ever my back was turned
             She did scandaliz' my name

SANDRA AND GETHYN: Now do you call that a sister?
No, no
You call that a sister?
No, no
Call that a sister?
No, no.
Scandaliz' my name.

SANDRA: Come on George.

GEORGE: Not me, can't swim, can't sing.

SANDRA AND GETHYN: I met my preacher the other day
I gave him my right hand
And just as soon
As ever my back was turned he do
Scandaliz' my name.

Now do you call that religion?
No, no!

RON enters, carrying a cauliflower. He's had a few pints of beer.
They stop singing.

SANDRA: Ron! This is Ron, my foreman at work. Meet
George…

RON: Not your foreman, my little beauty. Do you want the
good news or the bad news? Bad news is, half the jobs are
going. Good news is, they've made me manager, I get to
choose who goes.

SANDRA: You're joking?

RON: They like the way I handle the women, see George?

RON grabs SANDRA around her waist in a possessive gesture to GEORGE.

RON: Well then George, tell me all about yourself?

SANDRA: Gethyn, why not take your record player upstairs now?

GEORGE: Oh, I think I've bored them enough already. That's some cauliflower you got there, grow it yourself?

SANDRA: George brought Gethyn a present – a record.

RON: Did he now? Birthday, or something I don't know about?

SANDRA (*to GETHYN*): Go on, up you go.

GEORGE: Congratulations on your promotion. Well, thanks for the coffee.

RON glowers at SANDRA.

GEORGE: I'd better be going.

RON: Didn't she offer you some cake to go with it? Surprised, she's a good little cook, this one, aren't you? Amongst her other skills.

SANDRA: You've been drinking.

RON: Celebrating. I've brought us a bottle.

SANDRA: Thanks for the record, George.

GEORGE: No problem.

RON: I'll see you out.

GEORGE and RON go to the door. RON is hard faced. GEORGE knows what to expect.

RON: I don't know if you got the wrong impression George, but she's not free, understand?

GEORGE leaves.

RON: Why do you lie to me, Sandra? Why? Don't I do enough?

SANDRA: I had a spoonful of coffee left, what's the problem? He bought Gethyn a present.

RON: Oh, right, just like that. What is he then, the black Santa? I love you Sandra.

SANDRA: Oh, God.

RON: Why won't you believe me?

SANDRA: Here we go.

RON: I need you, Sand. I've been down the hospital all weekend, a hell of a time, the wife's arthritis...

SANDRA: Don't start talking about her!

RON: But I got to tell somebody! They took her in, put her on Morphine; told me she'll be in a wheel chair this time next year.

SANDRA: Every time you have a drink – I've heard it all before.

RON: But you should see her.

SANDRA: No you should see her! If you're so bothered about your wife, go and see her, but in my house you don't mention her understand?

RON: You're a heartless bitch sometimes.

SANDRA: And you're all heart Ron, really you are.

RON: You don't think I feel anything?

SANDRA: I didn't say that.

RON: Well I do see, 'cause I loved her.

SANDRA: But not anymore apparently.

RON: She was so beautiful when we got married. Never have thought it. Should have had kids, stupid, waited till we had the deposit on a house, weren't going to live on a council... but it was too late.

SANDRA: I've got a kid if you want one.

RON: When my sister brings her baby round... you can see it in her face. That's my life, Sand. That's all I got to look forward to, looking on at everyone else's lives...

'cept you, I look forward to you, ray of bloody sunshine you are.

SANDRA: Stop swearing.

RON: But I do Sandra, I love you. And this job, it's going to set us up fine. No one can sack you unless I say so. I'll give you all the best jobs, make you supervisor, how'd you like that, eh? Extra three pound a week, eh? What about that? Get yourself some new clothes with that eh? Buy the boy something if you want. Get him some more records eh? It's going to be good though Sandra, really good.

SANDRA: Supervisor?

RON: You want it?

SANDRA: Course I want it.

RON: Then you got it. See, see? I want to look after you. Hold me?

SANDRA does so.

RON: I'm sorry. So sorry.

SANDRA: There now, come on, it's all right.

They kiss. It becomes passionate, needy. SANDRA leads him off.

GETHYN remembers a scene from 'The Proud Valley'.

Projection: Down the pit, Emlyn Parry pauses, thinking of his father. Robeson stands beside him.

ROBESON: Penny for 'em Emlyn.

EMLYN: They're worth more than that, Dave.

Film ends.

GETHYN: George never came round again. Next time I saw him I was canoeing up the Essequibo River. 'Bloody crocodiles!'

GETHYN makes jungle animal sounds and imagines himself paddling. GEORGE is taking a stroll, singing 'Lazy Bones' from off-stage.

GEORGE (*singing*): Lazy bones, sleeping in the sun
How you expect to get your day's work
done
Never get your day's work done
Sleeping in the noon day sun

When taters need spraying
I bet you keep praying
The bugs fall off of the vine...

(*He enters, singing.*)

And when you go fishing
I bet you keep wishing
The fish won't grab at your line...

GETHYN (*as boy*): George!

GEORGE: Gethyn, my God boy, what you doing?

GETHYN (*as boy*): Building a canoe. See the river's black an' everything.

GEORGE (*slightly afraid*): Yeah.

GETHYN (*as boy*): You was singing.

GEORGE: I was not.

GETHYN (*as boy*): Yes you were.

GEORGE: Not me, boy.

GETHYN (*as boy*): You're not supposed to lie to children, it sets us a bad example.

GEORGE: Is that right?

GETHYN (*as boy*): I thought you was Paul Robeson for a minute.

GEORGE: I'm not that good.

GETHYN (*as boy*): See it was you. That's all right, I won't laugh.

GEORGE: Thanks.

GETHYN (*as boy*): I knew you'd like it once you started.

GEORGE: So what's this?

GETHYN (*as boy*): My canoe.

GEORGE: Got more holes than the Titanic.

GETHYN (*as boy*): Will you help me?

GEORGE: You need a tall tree, not corrugated iron.

GETHYN (*as boy*): Will you though?

GEORGE: Let's see. Got room for me?

GETHYN (*as boy*): Loads. I was just heading for a village, pick up supplies.

GEORGE and GETHYN get in the 'canoe'.

GEORGE: We're gonna need 'em!

GETHYN (*as boy*): See, I got my own paddle.

GEORGE: Pass me that old bit o'wood. Ready? Don't forget I can't swim.

GETHYN (*as boy*): That's all right, neither can I.

GEORGE: Great!

GETHYN (*as boy*): What shall we sing?

GEORGE: Got to be, there's only one song.

GETHYN (*as boy*): What's that?

GEORGE: The Canoe Song.

They start to sing as they play going up the river.

BOTH: I-ee-o-co
I-yo-co (x 2)

I ee ico Ye-ged-air
I ee ico Ye-ged-air
I ee ico, I ee ico, I ee ico.

SANDRA approaches to get GETHYN. Instead, she hides and watches them. The song becomes a four part harmony.

BOTH: I ee ico Ye-ged-air
I ee ico Ye-ged-air
The current swings, the water sings, a river rhyme.

For light is a burden of labour
When each bends his back with his neighbour
So peace for all,
We stand or fall,
And all for each,
Until we reach
The journey's end.

GETHYN (*as boy*): How come they don't sing in Guyana?

GEORGE: They do, all the time.

GETHYN (*as boy*): Then how come you didn't?

GEORGE: Just never did. My father wasn't one for music, he preferred the sound of machines. Me, well, I was the oldest son so I had to follow in his footsteps.

GEORGE starts singing again. GETHYN joins in.

BOTH: I ee oco, I ee oco, I ee oco.
　　　I ee oco, I ee oco, I ee oco.
　　　Standing-a-strong, standing-a-wise,
　　　Righter of wrong, hater of lies,
　　　Laughed as he fought, worked as he played,
　　　As he has taught, let it be made.
　　　Away you go Ye-ged-air,
　　　And make it so Ye-ged-air,
　　　Together all the paddles fall in tune and time,

GETHYN (*as boy*): Were your ancestors slaves then?

GEORGE: That's right.

GETHYN (*as boy*): Paul Robeson's father was a slave.

GEORGE: So I read, escaped though. Brave man.

GETHYN (*as boy*): Paul says that he's an African, really. Are you?

GEORGE: Yes, now I think maybe I am, a Guyanese African.

GETHYN (*as boy*): Have you been to Africa?

GEORGE: No.

GETHYN (*as boy*): Let's go there now.

GEORGE: The Maputo River.

GETHYN (*as boy*): Where's that?

GEORGE: South East Africa. That's where we think my great, great grandfather came from. See, he spoke Portuguese and they colonised that part of Africa.

GETHYN (*as boy*): What's it like?

GEORGE: I don't know.

GETHYN (*as boy*): Tell me about him?

GEORGE: That's all I know. There's nothing, no history books. Sometimes even my own family don't want to talk about it! S'like they're ashamed or something!

GETHYN (*as boy*): Same here.

GEORGE: But we shouldn't be ashamed should we, you and me? Our people have built these great countries with their blood and sweat, and do you know what? A part of this country belongs to us!

GETHYN (*as boy*): That's right! My Da could've died down the pit.

GEORGE: And what do we get left with eh? A river black with sorrow.

GETHYN (*as boy*): Like Big Glyn's bucket.

GEORGE: Guess we just better keep paddling.

GETHYN (*as boy*): The Kaiteur Falls is just ahead, the heartbeat of the world.

GEORGE: We're going to have to beat these damned alligators!

They whack imaginary alligators with their paddles – a release of tension.

GETHYN (*as boy*): Get 'em!

GEORGE: Come on, come on! We're afraid of nothing!

GETHYN (*as boy*): Look out!

GEORGE: I got it. There's another!

GETHYN (*as boy*): Kill! Kill!

GEORGE: Nothing's going to stop us!

GETHYN (*as boy*): Nothing!

GEORGE: We're a team!

They sing at the top of their voices, as they resume 'paddling'.

BOTH: So look alive Ye-ged-air,
   And dip and drive Ye-ged-air,
   The current swings, the water sings, a river rhyme.
   For light is the burden of labour
   When each bends his back with his neighbour
   So peace for all,
   We stand or fall,
   And all for each,
   Until we reach,
   The journey's end.

SANDRA (*approaching*): Geth.

GETHYN (*as boy*): Mam. Look it's George.

SANDRA: So I see.

GEORGE: Just helping Geth build a...

SANDRA: Your tea is getting fed up waiting for you, says it's going to jump into the frying pan and turn into bubble and squeak unless you come home right now.

GETHYN (*as boy*): I like bubble and squeak.

SANDRA: No you don't.

GEORGE: Best tie the canoe up to a tree don't want it floating off without you.

GETHYN (*as boy*): Right. Mam, can I bring my paddle home?

SANDRA: If you must.

GETHYN ties up his 'canoe'.

GEORGE: How are you?

SANDRA: Fine thanks. Come on Gethyn.

GEORGE: Job going okay?

SANDRA: Yes. Got promoted.

GEORGE: Congratulations. Every little helps eh?

49

SANDRA: That's right. Geth, get a move on.

GEORGE: Next Sunday, it's our national day in Guyana. I was going to cook some yams and breadfruit, rice, a glass of rum and coke to wash it down. Can't really celebrate on my own. I thought perhaps you and Gethyn could...

SANDRA: Sunday's my only day to do the washing. Come on Geth.

GEORGE: Sure. You're doing a fine job bringing up that boy.

SANDRA: And that's the way it's going to stay.

SANDRA walks away with the imaginary Gethyn. GEORGE is left alone.

GEORGE (*singing*): Drink to me only with thine eyes
                              And I shall pledge with mine. (*He exits.*)

Projection: A clip from 'The Proud Valley'. Emlyn at home, round the table.

MRS PARRY: My boy not good enough for her Gwen!

EMLYN: Mam, we may as well face it she was right.

MRS PARRY: Right? What do you mean?

EMLYN: We're finished, scrapped and finished.

MRS PARRY: But my boy...

EMLYN: It's no use Mum, there's nothing more to say!

50

Robeson thinks, hatches a plan and smiles.

Film ends.

SANDRA hugs GETHYN and sings. They are snoozy and relaxed.

SANDRA (*singing*): This little light of mine I'm going to let
                                                    it shine (x 3)
                                Let it shine, let it shine, let it shine
                                All through the night I'm going to let it
                                                                shine (x 2)
                                All through the night let it shine,
                                Let it shine, let it shine...

Ron's motorbike interrupts the song.

RON: Sandra?! Sand?!

SANDRA: We're in here.

RON: Oh. A bit late for him to be up isn't it?

SANDRA: No.

RON: Don't mollycoddle the boy like that.

SANDRA: What?

RON: I don't know, it's...

SANDRA: It's what?

RON: I dunno.

SANDRA: Ah, poor Ron, his mother never cwtshed him.

RON: Shut up.

SANDRA: Big baby.

RON: Shut up.

SANDRA: Go on Geth give Ron a cwtsh.

RON and GETHYN freeze with dread. There is a tense pause.

RON: Don't have to.

GETHYN (*as boy*): Ta.

SANDRA: The pair of you!

RON: You're turning him daft.

SANDRA (*suddenly harsh*): Don't tell me how to bring up my son!

RON: I'm only saying...

SANDRA: Drop it.

RON: Well you are! All this baloney... see, I didn't swear.

SANDRA: You nearly did.

RON: Ah, but I didn't. All this baloney about Paul Robeson, and his Da dying in the war. I mean...

SANDRA: Drop it now!

GETHYN (*as boy*): What Ma?

SANDRA: Nothing, he's drunk.

RON: I haven't so much as smacked my lips.

SANDRA (*to GETHYN*): Go to bed.

GETHYN (*as boy*): What's he saying?

SANDRA: Nothing. He's just an ignorant man.

RON: Hey, watch it.

SANDRA (*shouting*): Go to bed!

GETHYN (*as boy*): But I haven't done anything...

SANDRA: I know baby, it's all right. Please just go on up. Put your record on. I'll be up those stairs before he gets to the chorus.

GETHYN (*as boy*): All right Mam.

They wait for GETHYN to go.

GETHYN: Top of the stairs, shoes off, sneak back down to listen.

SANDRA: How dare you interfere like that.

RON: Well, for God's sake Sandra, half the valley knows he's a bastard, how long before his school mates do?

SANDRA: He's not a bastard, he's mine. It's what he believes in that counts.

RON: It's what he is that counts round here. Ask your mother.

SANDRA: You keep her out of this. That old bitch can go and rot in hell for all I care. (*She sings at RON:*)
>Call that religion, No, no!
>Scandaliz' my name!

RON: You're all barking! He's illegitimate, a bastard, call it what you like, he's got to know sooner or later.

SANDRA: He's a little boy! He's got to believe in something. He's got to have something that allows him to walk down that street with his head up.

RON: But why a pack of lies?

SANDRA: How do you know it's lies? You didn't know his father.

RON: Did you?

SANDRA slaps him.

RON: Christ Sandra, I'm sorry, really I am, I didn't mean it. I knew I was wrong, I just, I could hear the words coming out of my mouth and my brain's like, telling me, 'No, don't say that!' Sorry love... and the boy too. I won't say anything. I mean, it's not as if I want to get involved anyhow. He's yours, that's right, and you bring him up any way you see fit. I don't want to know. I'll just stay out of his way from now on all right? All right? He's a good lad really. You know how I am, just makes me uneasy, like, him around. You know I can't help it, can I? Thinking of you with another man whenever I see him. It's only 'cause I love you so much. I want you all to myself, see? For ever, past and present like, in't it? I'll stay out of his way.

SANDRA: Yes, stay out of his way.

RON: Suppose you'll be wanting to tuck him in then?

SANDRA: Yes.

RON: I'll go off then, see if I can catch a pint down the Marquis. I know I'm clumsy. I don't need telling. Tell him I was stinking drunk, thought he was someone else. I wouldn't hurt anyone, you know that.

SANDRA: Don't want to talk anymore now, Ron.

RON: You're right, said too much already.

SANDRA: I never knew you felt like that about Gethyn.

RON: Like what? What did I say?

SANDRA: Have you ever spoken to him?

RON: Look I said, didn't I?

SANDRA: Yep, you said. Goodnight.

RON: Night.

RON goes. SANDRA goes as if to Gethyn's bedroom. He has gone.

SANDRA: Geth? Gethyn? Where are you? Geth! Oh, my God!

Sound of Ron's motorbike starting.

GETHYN: Out the window, down the drain pipe, picked up my paddle, went into the street, hid and waited. One swipe of his foot and the engine started, squeeze the clutch, toe down, kicks into first, revs up a notch and away with the clutch. Smooth as you like he comes towards me, a single light in the dark of the Essequibo river. Crocodile roaring. Mouth open. I balance in my canoe and swing that paddle as hard as I can!

GETHYN swings his paddle, as if at RON. The sound of Ron's motorbike crashing.

Lights down on stage.

Projection: A clip from 'The Proud Valley'. Dick Parry is holding choir practice when Emlyn arrives late, after a fight at work.

DICK : Emlyn come here. Was it a good scrap son?

EMLYN: Aye Dad.

DICK: Good boy!

Film ends.

Blackout.

Act Two

Sunday. GEORGE is sitting at home, alone, listening to Robeson sing 'Gloomy Sunday'.

Robeson: Sadly one Sunday I waited and waited,
With flowers in my arms for a dream I'd created,
I waited till dreams like my heart were all broken,
The flowers were all dead and the words were
unspoken.
The grief that I knew was beyond all consol...

GEORGE (*takes the record off*): Man!

SANDRA and GETHYN arrive, taking GEORGE by surprise. GETHYN is sullen; SANDRA is anxious.

GEORGE: You're here!

SANDRA: You asked us to dinner.

GEORGE: Yeah, but I...

SANDRA: Haven't you even started cooking yet?

GEORGE: No, I...

SANDRA: We're starving, aren't we boy?

GEORGE: Geth, hi. (*Realising something is wrong:*) You okay?

SANDRA: He's a bit quiet. Well, are you going to cook or not?

GEORGE: It'll take a while.

SANDRA: Need a hand?

GEORGE: Sure. (*To GETHYN:*) You gonna help too?

SANDRA: Let him sit for a bit.

GEORGE (*to GETHYN*): I got a new Paul Robeson record, do you want to hear it?

SANDRA: I should leave it if I were you. Put on the radio.

GEORGE: All right.

GEORGE mimes putting on the radio. A broadcast of 'Family Favourites' plays in the background. GEORGE and SANDRA cross stage, as if to the kitchen.

GEORGE: Something happened?

SANDRA: Don't ask.

GEORGE: You want a drink?

SANDRA: Hm.

GEORGE pours her a rum and coke.

GEORGE: It's supposed to have ice, but... I can't work it out, we can make ice in the Caribbean, but you lot – in this freezing wet – no hope!

SANDRA is trying to hide her distress.

GEORGE: You want to sit down? I can do it.

SANDRA: No, give me something to do, for God's sake.

GEORGE: You can start with the yams.

GEORGE hands SANDRA a yam.

SANDRA: What in God's name is that?!

GEORGE: You wait, just you wait and see.

GETHYN: Heavy net curtains to keep out the eyes. Diffused white light on the dark rented furniture. And something new, on the wall: a picture torn from a magazine – National Geographic; the Kaiteur Falls. The heat beat of the world, stopped dead. 'Family Favourites' on the radio.

The song 'Strangers in Paradise' is heard.

Time has passed.

SANDRA: They wouldn't let Ron out of the hospital till this morning. Gethyn won't say a word.

GEORGE: What have you told him?

SANDRA: I don't know how much he heard, do I?

GEORGE: Maybe he should hear it all.

SANDRA: You don't know the half of it. To start with, I never was married.

GEORGE shrugs.

SANDRA: You could try and act surprised. Am I that obvious? He was a passing stranger. Not that he was my first, mind. Sang in a band, American forces, played cornet as well. New faces in town, wan'it. All us girls were down the front, like kids at a sweet shop window and not a farthing between us. But he took a shine, see, took a shine to me, winked and smiled. Katherine my mate, was going, 'Ooh, see that? The cheeky beggar.' Mirror ball swirling in my head, and me: Jean Harlow on the dance floor. He was only here one night, he was off to Swansea next morning. Gave me his address, but I never got a reply. Cincinnati. My mother said I must be stupid, it was obvious he was the devil! Who else would come from a place called Cin-cin-nati.

GEORGE: And the Paul Robeson thing?

SANDRA: That bit's true. He told me he'd sung with Paul Robeson in a show on Broadway. They were friends.

GETHYN: Then it happened.

ROBESON (*from the radio*): 'Sometimes I feel like a motherless child, a long way from my home.'

GETHYN (*as boy*): Lying, you're all lying!

Projection: A clip from 'The Proud Valley'. Nick wants to get through to stranded miners. The music is simultaneous.

NICK: I'll smash a way through, I'll smash a way through!

ROBESON: Steady Nick, steady.

GETHYN: Radio, bakelite, brown, in my hands, above my head.

GEORGE: No!

SANDRA: Gethyn!!

GETHYN mimes smashing the radio on the floor.

The film ends. Silence.

GETHYN: I never meant it to explode like that, scared the hell out of me. Course I couldn't admit it, so I made out I meant it.

GETHYN (*as boy*): Serves you right! Serves you all right!

SANDRA: I'm so sorry, I'll pay for the damage. For God's sake, Gethyn. I'll get you home. George, forgive me.

GEORGE: Look, hang on a second! Let me get this cleared up.

SANDRA: Of course, I'm sorry, I'll do it, get me a dustpan and brush.

GEORGE: No! I mean get *this* cleared up! Now listen here young man, this is my home. It maybe a crummy bedsit, but it's my place and no matter what you got going on in your head, when you come here you treat me with respect, you understand? You don't go smashing up the place like you owned it. Mind where you tread! Now we are going to clear this mess up together and put things back in their place. Don't anybody move! I'll get the broom.

GETHYN: We both stood, unable to look at one another, in this sea of shattered valves, copper wires and casing – jagged, lethal. One wrong step and the blood would flow.

GEORGE: Right, you (*to GETHYN*) – the brush. You (*to SANDRA*) – the dustpan. I'll take the broom, if no one objects!

GETHYN and SANDRA squat down and begin sweeping. They do not make eye contact.

GEORGE: What did Paul Robeson do wrong? Nothing! All he did was sing with your father.

GETHYN looks up in hope.

GEORGE (*to SANDRA*): Haven't you told him anything? (*To GETHYN:*) That much is true, kid, your father sang with Paul Robeson in a show on Broadway – that's in New York, America, USA, only the best play there. And they were friends.

GETHYN looks at SANDRA – she still can't look at him.

SANDRA: It's true.

GEORGE: What else about him?

SANDRA: How do you mean?

GEORGE: What colour hair did he have?

SANDRA: Dark.

GEORGE: Eyes?

62

SANDRA: Brown.

GEORGE: Height?

SANDRA: Six foot.

GEORGE: Good looking?

SANDRA: Absolutely gorgeous.

GEORGE: Could he sing?

SANDRA: Like a dream.

GEORGE: What else could he do?

SANDRA: Play the cornet.

GEORGE: What did people think of him?

SANDRA: They loved him, adored him, never seen the place swing like it did that night.

GEORGE: Did you?

SANDRA: What?

GEORGE: Did you love him?

SANDRA: I was just a girl.

GEORGE: Answer the boy.

SANDRA (*finally, she looks at GETHYN*): Yes, I loved him. I felt like Cinderella. Like someone had given me wings to fly with. I've never been so in love as that night; my one night.

GEORGE: You only spent one night together?

SANDRA: Yes.

GEORGE: And from that you had Gethyn?

SANDRA: Yes.

GEORGE: That's makes him pretty special don't it?

SANDRA: A miracle.

GEORGE: Wouldn't have it any other way?

SANDRA: No. It was the most perfect night of my life and it gave me the most perfect son.

GETHYN (*as boy*): What was his name?

SANDRA: Dean.

GEORGE: Like Dean Martin!

GETHYN (*as boy*): What was his other name?

SANDRA doesn't know. She looks to GEORGE for help.

GEORGE: Just Dean, man, like in Cinderella, the Prince only had one name.

GETHYN (*as boy*): What?

GEORGE: Charming.

GETHYN (*as boy*): Oh yeah.

GEORGE: Mind your fingers. Right now...

GETHYN (*as boy*): I'm sorry.

GEORGE: I know, kid, I know. It just frightened me, that's all, I thought you was blaming me for something...

GETHYN (*as boy; starting to cry*): No, I don't...

GEORGE holds out his hand to GETHYN.

GEORGE: Still friends then?

GETHYN: I cried – inconsolable, they call it. Water falling from my eyes, eight hundred feet straight down, 'highest waterfall in the world man, highest waterfall in the world'.

GEORGE and SANDRA sit, stuffed after the meal.

SANDRA: I've never tasted anything like it.

GEORGE: Reckon I should start my own business?

SANDRA: No, couldn't eat that out of newspaper, go all soggy.

GEORGE: I could taste home in every mouthful. Could see my house, the ocean, Georgetown on market day, the women buying cloth, kids stealing fruit from their baskets.

GEORGE becomes tearful. GETHYN sees.

GETHYN (*as boy*): Mam?

SANDRA: You all right George?

GEORGE: That's just the rum welling up in my eyes. I was thinking of my mother. She died when I was six years-old. She was kind of round if you know what I mean? Big, and she swung when she walked, but she swung proud, you know, 'Here I am and I love eating!' When father was away building roads – and roads and roads – she and the other women would come to the house and put on the radio and dance. Man! Us kids would sit on the sofa and giggle till we cried. All the women dancing and imitating the men, howling and... my mother, she swung those hips, boy, could shake the nails out the roof! Then she'd sit and fan she self and call for lemonade like it was somebody's fault she'd laughed so much. But when my father was home, that was it. Silent and it stayed that way after her death, forever silent. I miss her. You're a lucky boy Geth. What in the Lord's name got me going about that?

SANDRA: The food.

GEORGE: Yes. (*Sings:*) 'Every time I feel the spirit
Moving in my heart I will pray,
Yes every time, every time,
I feel the spirit, I feel the spirit,
Moving in my heart now I will pray.'

SANDRA: Thought you couldn't sing?

GEORGE: Ah, well you see, I couldn't, till this boy came snooping at me window wanting me to sing! First I chased him with a cricket bat, 'There's no way I'm gonna sing!' said I. Then he told me all about his daddy's friend, Paul

Robeson, and how he sang and spoke of a better world where every person no matter what, or who they are, is special. And it got me thinking about why I never sang, and then I realised I'd always sung, just never let the sounds out before that's all. So I let the sounds out, loud as hell, bouncing off the walls back at me. First time I'd ever been surrounded by my own sound and I knew then why the little boy wanted me to sing. So now... (*he sings:*) Every time I feel the spirit moving in my heart I will pray!

They all sing. GETHYN watches SANDRA and GEORGE as they dance. Their dance slows.

Projection: A clip from 'The Proud Valley', of Emlyn and Gwen at Emlyn's house.

SANDRA and GEORGE dance through the film.

GWEN: Emlyn let's get married

EMLYN: What on my dole money, with my mother and the kids on public assistance and things getting worse every week?

GWEN: Emlyn those things don't matter, plenty of people in Blaendy who get married like that.

EMLYN: Aye it's easy enough to get married but what about the future?

GWEN: We'd be facing it together

EMLYN: And bringing up our children on two bob a week, it's not good enough.

GWEN: I'm telling you it's good enough for me.

EMLYN: I like your spirit, lovely. I'm as anxious to get married as you are.

GWEN: My own boy.

Film ends.

GETHYN: Come evening, warm voices chatter in the ether, swirl in the room above your head. Gentle tones and laughter. Bass vibrations and soothing alto murmurings, touched upon the air like stroking hands.

GEORGE: He's asleep. Been through a lot today.

SANDRA: I'm going to have to wake him up to get him home.

GEORGE: I'll carry him.

SANDRA: Wrap him in my coat.

GEORGE: Take mine, he likes it.

SANDRA: Is there anything he doesn't like about you? Me, I've never seen such hatred in his eyes.

GEORGE: As long as he knows that he's loved; if he doesn't know that then he'll grow bitter and that'll take him a lifetime to shift. Knowing he's loved is more important than anything else he hasn't got. I envy him you.

SANDRA: How can you say that?

GEORGE: Because you love him, and will do anything for him.

SANDRA: I'm proud of him.

GEORGE: Of course you are.

SANDRA: I think he's beautiful.

GEORGE: He is.

SANDRA: Thank you for today.

GEORGE: Why did you come?

SANDRA: I was thinking earlier, 'Why on earth did I bring him today of all days?' And I think it was just out of instinct. I knew I couldn't handle it on my own and... it's the first time, well no, that's a lie, it's not the first time, but it was one time that I really needed his father here.

GEORGE: I'm flattered.

SANDRA: Don't be, you'd make a great Dad.

GEORGE: No way, that's not for me. We should go.

They wrap an imaginary Gethin in GEORGE's coat. GEORGE Picks him up in his arms.

GETHYN: Half awake, sleep pulling you into his chest, can't go to sleep, don't want to miss this feeling, don't want to miss... don't want... don't...

They sing 'My Curly-Headed Baby' as they 'Walk Home to Sandra's House'. GEORGE and SANDRA enjoy the song and make each other laugh.

GEORGE and SANDRA: Oh my baby, my curly-headed baby
                           I'll sing you fast asleep
                           And love you so as I sing

                           Oh my baby, my curly-headed baby
                           Just tuck your head like little bird
                           Beneath its mother's wing

                           So Lulla-Lulla, Lulla-Lulla, bye-bye
                           Do you want the stars to play with
                           Or the moon to run away with
                           They'll come if you don't cry

                           So Lulla-Lulla, Lulla-Lulla, bye-bye
                           To your mother's arms be creeping
                           And soon you'll be a'sleeping
                           Lulla, Lulla-Lulla, Lulla-Lulla,
                                               bye...

RON appears, bandaged.

RON: Where the hell have you been?

SANDRA: Ssh! Can't you see he's asleep.

RON: Asleep is it? I'll give him asleep. (*Referring to GEORGE:*)
And what's he doing here?

SANDRA (*to GEORGE*): Just get him inside.

RON: Oi! I'm talking to you. I said...

SANDRA: There, you've woken him! Here I'll take him.

SANDRA takes the imaginary Gethyn from GEORGE.

RON: Have you seen what he's done to my front forks?

SANDRA: Ron, go home.

SANDRA goes.

RON: She been with you all day has she?

GEORGE: The boy was upset.

RON: The boy was upset? Never mind me then? He'll be bloody upset when I get my hands on him.

GEORGE: May be you should go and calm down.

RON: Me? You're telling me to go?

GEORGE: I'm not looking for trouble.

RON: I don't think you got the picture.

GEORGE: I got the picture.

RON: No, I don't think you have. I'm her boss, get it?

GEORGE: I get it. Like you said, the woman ain't free.

SANDRA returns.

SANDRA: Ron, go home. We'll discuss this in the morning.

RON: What about him?

SANDRA: You'll miss the bus.

RON: The bus?

SANDRA: Well, how else you going to get home? You haven't got your motorbike. Last one goes on the hour.

RON (*checks his watch*): Damn!

SANDRA: She'll be wondering where you are.

RON: Damn that child! Your mother's right, he's the devil's spawn! I'll see you at work. And don't be late! And I don't want to see you again, boyo.

RON has to run for the bus.

SANDRA: Run! Never think he used to be a scrum half would you? (*She laughs.*) Right then, cup of Coffee?

GEORGE: No. I'll be going. Thanks all the same.

SANDRA: Please.

GEORGE: I got work tomorrow, roads to build, you know how it is.

SANDRA: I want you to stay.

GEORGE: I don't know.

SANDRA: Yes you do. (*She kisses him.*)

GEORGE: Look, stop. I can't do this.

SANDRA: Why not?

GEORGE: I just can't, all right?

SANDRA: Why not?

GEORGE: Look, I'm here to do this contract. I build the road then go. An' I'm thinking, yeah, why not, never have to see her again, it'd be very comfortable, you know? But you don't need that, neither of you need that. Besides, what if it turned into more than that?

SANDRA: What if it did?

GEORGE: No. It can't.

SANDRA: Why not?

GEORGE: A whole host of reasons! Firstly, firstly, just us. You don't need any more tongues wagging – and going with a black guy, well! And me, no, I don't need this going on. I'm alone here, got me? I just want to be invisible and I'm finding that very difficult, you know what I mean? They don't like the fact that I'm the engineer and they're the labourers. It's bad enough getting them to listen to what I say, I have to earn their respect and prove everything twice over before they'll do anything! You telling me that being with a white woman, one of their own, is going to make that any easier? No. We both got our lives and our jobs to keep, when I leave we'll still have them, that's the way it's got to be.

SANDRA: Well I'm not going to beg.

GEORGE: Sandra... I'd fall in love with you, I probably already am falling, I have, I don't know, but it can't be. I'm not saying that I don't want you. Just let us be friends. We are friends, good friends aren't we? After today, I mean...?

SANDRA: Yes.

GEORGE: Then let's keep that.

SANDRA: Can I come round?

GEORGE: Sure.

SANDRA: And you'll come here?

GEORGE: Invite me.

They part and exit. SANDRA smiles.

GETHYN: I was happy with that, see. I knew my Mam wasn't going to give up that easy. Besides, I'd seen 'The Proud Valley', I knew 'women got their ways'.

Projection: A clip from 'The Proud Valley', where Gwen comes to Emlyn's house in her new dress. (Meanwhile, SANDRA and GEORGE get changed into fashionable fifties' clothes.)

EMLYN: Hello lovely.

GWEN: Hello Em.

EMLYN: You look great!

GWEN: Like it?

EMLYN: You bet!

GWEN: Hello everybody.

PHYLLIS: Hello Gwen!

SISTER: Doesn't she look nice. Hoping to win the Eisteddfod, Gwen?

PHYLLIS: Don't be silly it isn't a beauty competition.

BROTHER: Are they sunflowers?

PHYLLIS: It's very nice, but it's a bit on the short side.

Film ends.

GETHYN: Before George's visits, Mam'd spend ages in the bathroom and come out smelling like the ground floor of a department store. Lovely! I was that proud of her.

SANDRA: How do I look, Geth?

GETHYN looks on, adoring and speechless.

SANDRA: That good, eh? That's my boy.

GETHYN: And George? Never without a white shirt, suit and tie, and his shoes! What shoes! Tapped as he walked, click-click-clickerty-scuff. Mine wouldn't do it, tried for ages. But more, a different flower in his buttonhole every time and he never once left our house with it.

Robeson sings 'River Stay 'Way From My Door'. SANDRA and GEORGE dance. GEORGE puts a flower in SANDRA's hair.

Projection: The clip from 'The Proud Valley', of Robeson thinking, then hatching a plan, is shown again.

GETHYN mirrors Robeson's expression.

Film ends.

GETHYN interrupts SANDRA and GEORGE's flirting.

GETHYN (*as boy*): I got a letter home from school. They's asking parents to do something at the Eisteddfod again.

SANDRA: Oh.

GETHYN (*as boy*): Come on Mam, we never do anything.

SANDRA: No, and I'm not going to this year either.

GETHYN (*as boy*): Why not?

GEORGE: Yes, why not?

SANDRA: I'm not standing up in front of that lot, with them all thinking... well, let them think, I'm not doing it.

GETHYN (*as boy*): Come on Mam, you sing lovely.

GEORGE: Lovely.

SANDRA: I'm not doing it.

GEORGE: Stand up there and sing with the boy, what harm can it do?

GETHYN (*as boy*): Go on Mam. George will if you will.

GEORGE: What?

SANDRA: Really? Oh, well then, I will if George will.

GEORGE: Now, wait a second.

GETHYN (*as boy*): You will won't you George? The three of us?

SANDRA: Well, Georgie boy? Don't want to let the boy down do we?

GEORGE: You are the...

GETHYN (*as boy*): Yes, just say yes.

GEORGE: Yes.

SANDRA: No, you can't say 'yes'.

GEORGE: I just have.

SANDRA: You can't!

GEORGE: Got you now haven't I?

SANDRA: No!

GEORGE: Too late, you said it. You're getting up on that stage!

SANDRA: Please.

GETHYN (*as boy*): Too late, too late.

GEORGE: Ah-ha! Now whose in a jam?

SANDRA: You...

GEORGE: Now, now, not in front of the child.

SANDRA: Happy now?

GETHYN (*as boy*): Yes.

SANDRA: Oh, my God. What are we going to sing?

GETHYN (*as boy*): 'Sandaliz' my name!'

SANDRA: Maybe not this time. We'll have a think, meanwhile, you off to bed, mister. Go on before I change my mind.

GETHYN goes.

SANDRA: Are you really going to do it?

GEORGE: Why not? Doesn't mean anything.

SANDRA: People might see it otherwise.

GEORGE: You think so?

SANDRA: Might.

GEORGE: What like?

SANDRA: Like we're a family

GEORGE kisses SANDRA.

GEORGE: That wasn't meant to happen.

SANDRA: No, I wonder if it will happen again.

They kiss again, then hear RON arrive on his motorbike.

RON: Not interrupting something, am I?

SANDRA: No, no, course not. Gethyn's just getting into his pyjamas.

RON: Bike's fixed.

SANDRA: How much did it cost?

RON: Don't matter.

SANDRA: No, really, I'll pay.

RON: Don't matter I said. (*He makes himself at home.*) Put the kettle on love, you know how I like it. (*To GEORGE:*) Don't mind me.

SANDRA: George was just leaving.

GEORGE: Was I?

SANDRA: Getting late. For the best.

GEORGE: I see. Pardon me.

SANDRA: I'll see you out.

GEORGE: No bother.

SANDRA: It's all right.

SANDRA and GEORGE step out of the house.

SANDRA: George, wait.

GEORGE: What for? Are you going to? With him? Is that what he's here for? What are you the slave owner's woman? Well, I'm not a slave and I'm not standing by watching my woman be degraded by his touch.

SANDRA: Now you wait here.

GEORGE: He's right, you know, you're not free.

SANDRA: You haven't had to bring a child up alone. Don't get self-righteous with me! You've been to university, got a degree, what have I got? Don't you dare lecture me!

GEORGE: Forget it, you're right, what do I know, or care, I'm outa here soon.

SANDRA: George.

GEORGE goes. SANDRA goes inside.

RON: Little tiff?

SANDRA: No.

RON: These Sambo's got tempers mind, wanna be careful. I'll pick you up for work in the morning eh? My girl don't have to get the bus. Put the kettle on. Been missing you. Thinking about you. Drives me crazy. Can't sleep at night, know what I mean? You too I'll bet. What's up? He upset you? I'll have a word!

SANDRA: No! Sit down. Ron, sit down.

RON does so.

SANDRA: I can't do this any longer. You understand me?

RON: Sand...

SANDRA: You think I can't feel them twitching at their curtains as I walk down the street, thinking, 'Hard bitch, she's got a mouth on her considering what she gets up to'. See it's all right for you isn't it? Come in here get your leg over, cup of tea, talk about your wife. Tell me I'm not a slag, go on, an easy lay.

RON: Who's been saying that?

SANDRA: I saw sparkling lights, and something beautiful, it was waiting for me, I was certain, absolutely bloody certain. I thought I had it once, for a moment, but the clock struck twelve and all I had was my knickers round my ankles. You aren't ever going to be the one for me Ron, you can't be my husband. You'll never, ever, want to be Gethyn's Da.

RON: Is this to do with that Negro?

SANDRA: No! This isn't what I want. When I look forward now all I see is this. Sitting indoors waiting for you to come round. Five minutes of betrayal, disgusting, despicable isn't it? And you're gone. Tell me you don't feel guilty? Go on, tell me? 'Cause I do, by God I feel like scum. And do you know what? I hate her – Betty, your arthritic, ex-Miss Rhondda. I hate her because she makes me feel so low, just the fact that she exists is more than I can bear. But I can't hate her, not really, it's me, I hate, me! And then what have I got? Work, and work, and work, till I can't stand the minutes of my life. I hate and resent each one because it takes so long to die. All those minutes that have died in me. The only thing I've done remotely right, was love that boy. And you can't stand the sight of him. I want us to be friends Ron. God knows I've listened to enough of your problems to be your mother, but I'll be your friend, but no more, no more coming round here and making love to me. 'No more, no more'.

RON: I'll leave her.

SANDRA: No, no.

RON: I will.

SANDRA: No. I don't want you to Ron. I don't want you.

RON (*gets up to leave*): What have I got? Without you I've got nothing.

SANDRA: They'll be other factory girls.

RON: Is that what you think? Well in that case, don't bother coming to work tomorrow! You can collect your cards from the office on Friday.

SANDRA expected as much. GETHYN sings 'No More Auction Block For Me'. Lights change. SANDRA exits.

Projection: A clip from 'The Proud Valley'.

Simultaneously, a choreographed dance/fight takes place, in which GEORGE is brutally attacked by RON.

GETHYN: No more auction block for me, no more, no more.
　　　　　No more auction block for me,
　　　　　Many thousand gone.

　　　　　No more pint of salt for me, no more, no more.
　　　　　No more pint of salt for me,
　　　　　Many thousand gone.

　　　　　No more driver's lash for me, no more, no more,
　　　　　No more driver's lash for me,
　　　　　Though many thousand gone,
　　　　　Freedom we will have.

SETH: This fellow brought a black man to work down the pit!

ROBESON: Well, what about it?

DICK PARRY: All right David, leave me to deal with him. Now listen lads, Dave here is more than a good singer, he's as good a Butty as ever worked down a pit with me. Aye, and he's a decent chap into the bargain. Here's Seth talking about him being black, Well damn and blast it! Aren't we all black down that pit.

EMLYN: Aye take a look at yourselves. This fellow's as good a pal as any of you.

DICK PARRY: Well, anybody got anything to say before me and my Butty go down the pit?

GEORGE is left battered. SANDRA FINDS him and cares for him. As the song and film end, lights change to her house. He pulls away from her.

GEORGE: What you going to do?

SANDRA: Whatever you want to do?

GEORGE: You don't get the messages other people send out do you? What is it, faulty receiver or what? Maybe that's what happened with Dean? What is it with you? I get beaten, you lose your job, and now Gethyn is suffering and all we've done is kiss three times. A punishment for every one. Don't touch me! I knew this would happen, I knew it, I've been Black all my life why didn't I listen to myself!? I don't want to be no victim in your white society. And no, I'm not Paul Robeson! I can't come into your valleys and be a hero, I'm just George Cumberbatch – a nigger, not a celebrity. Yes, and do you know what? I'm proud of it and I don't want a white woman. That's right. I don't want one. Sure, I was curious, but it was never a status symbol thing with me. My father's right, for centuries your slave masters took our women and watered down our blood and I don't want to be a part of that 'great tradition'. So you make your plans, and I'll make mine! (*He regrets his words.*) Anything else is just going to bring us pain and suffering. It's not fair on either of us, our lives, it's not fair to trap each other with that and it certainly ain't fair on Gethyn.

SANDRA: You're a coward.

GEORGE: There you go again, not getting the message. Bang the side of your head! See if that helps! Go to the repair shop, get it seen to!

SANDRA: You're a coward. You never stood up to your father and you're not able to now. You've always been crushed. That's why you couldn't sing and why we can. No one crushes us.

GEORGE: Say goodbye to the kid for me.

SANDRA: See, you are a coward. You're going to walk out without saying goodbye. You, the great explainer, oh you can explain everyone else's mistakes, but you can't face your own. Go on then get out! I've had enough cowards in my life thank you. Get out! You'd only be a burden.

GEORGE goes. GETHYN walks in to the projected image of Robeson explaining to Emlyn.

ROBESON: Listen, son, your father was my friend. He took me in, gave me food and shelter, found me work. What kind of a man would I be if I left now when things are bad. Let's not talk about it now.

GEORGE is leaving with his small suitcase and a record. GETHYN approaches with the paddle. At first, GEORGE thinks GETHYN will hit him with it. GETHYN hands it to him, as Robeson sings 'The Canoe Song'. GEORGE writes his address down on the record, hands it to GETHYN, then goes.

GETHYN: And away he went, leaving me up the Essequibo without the vestige of a paddle. Word got out that Mam had been having affairs with Ron and a black man. Not sure which was worse in their eyes, but she couldn't get another job. Meanwhile Robeson was shunned in his country, his records were burned, his concerts banned, his words twisted and made perverse. I don't forgive easily, why should we?

SANDRA enters wearily and takes off her coat. There is the sound of a motorbike going passed.

SANDRA: I'll make the tea.

GETHYN (*as boy*): What we got?

SANDRA: Bubble and squeak.

GETHYN pulls a face. SANDRA sits down and looks, as if out of the window.)

SANDRA: Give me a minute.

GETHYN watches SANDRA. She becomes aware.

SANDRA: Don't worry. I'm all right.

GETHYN (*as boy*): I'm sorry.

SANDRA: What for?

GETHYN (*as boy*): That George didn't want me.

SANDRA: George loved you Geth, it wan't you. It's the way the world is. It's not your doing. Now come here.

GETHYN (*as boy*): Will we ever see him again?

SANDRA: One day Geth, one day.

GETHYN (*as boy*): It's always 'one day'.

SANDRA cuddles GETHYN.

SANDRA: Is it? Well not today it isn't, I've got a little surprise for you. I wasn't going to tell you but, why not eh? We both need cheering up. The miners are all off to Porthcawl next week for their Eisteddfod and Mrs Big Glyn has asked if we'd like to go along. See, something very special has just happened.

GETHYN (*as boy*): What's that?

SANDRA: You know the telephone wires on the poles?

GETHYN (*as boy*): Yeah.

SANDRA: Well they made a huge one and laid it right under the Atlantic Ocean from America to here.

GETHYN (*as boy*): No!

SANDRA: Aye! Now we can talk to the Americans like they was in our own front rooms.

GETHYN (*as boy*): Wow!

SANDRA: So the miners are going to phone America and guess who they're going to talk to?

GETHYN (*as boy*): Dean?

SANDRA: No, no, they don't know Dean's phone number, but they're going to talk to Paul Robeson.

GETHYN (*as boy*): No!

SANDRA: And he's going to sing to us, and we're going to sing to him. You, young man are going to get the chance to sing with Paul Robeson!

GETHYN: Suddenly, there he was, my Da, just out of reach, finger tips away, we'll have both sung with Paul Robeson. He was that close, that close, I could hear his voice! This was it! My destiny! My happy, happy destiny.

Projection: A clip from 'The Proud Valley', of the train approaching and Robeson jumping in to a wagon.

Film ends.

GETHYN: Train ride down was something! 'Miners' Special' it said. Mrs Big Glyn sat Mam down by her, so's nobody would say anything. Men in baggy suits and women in cardies. Us lads Brylcreamed flat like our heads had been ironed. Girls in clusters of Candy Stripe and Bobby Socks. And Tizer, to make your tongue turn orange and burp up the taste of fish paste sandwiches. Aye, and hard boiled eggs to throw at passengers as we tore through their platforms on the way to Porthcawl.

Then, the hall, huge, never seen anything like it. Five thousand people all here to sing! To sing! It could only happen here, see? In Wales. I don't know, it's become fashionable to be embarrassed about it now, but I'm not, see. I'm just not.

They are now in the hall at Porthcawl.

SANDRA: Stay by me! If you get lost how am I meant to find you?

GETHYN: Then up he got, the Treorchy Male voice choir behind him, this tiny man, the great Will Paynter, our leader. Everyone knew that he had a brilliant mind and the hall fell silent and stared at him, as if by doing so we might see it. He stepped forward to the microphone, and looked out across us, but he was only talking to one man.

We hear the actual recording:

WILL PAYNTER: Hello Paul Robeson, this is Will Paynter, President of the South Wales Miners, speaking. On behalf of the South Wales Miners and all the people gathered at this Eisteddfod, I extend to you warm greetings of friendship and respect. We are happy that it has been possible for us to arrange for you to speak and to sing for us today, we would be far happier if you were with us to speak in person. Our people deplore the continued refusal of your government to return your passport and to deny you the right to join us in our festival of song. We shall continue to exert what influence we can to overcome this position. We look forward to the day when we shall again shake you by the hand and hear you sing with us in these valleys of music and song. Over to you Paul.

GETHYN: Was the phone line working? Had a shark bitten through it? Then out of the air itself, like a God...

Projection: During the following speech, a silent clip from 'The Proud Valley' is played. Robeson marches through the streets, as the community sing, 'They Can't Stop Us Singing'.

ROBESON: Thank you so much for your very kind words. My warmest greeting to the people of my beloved Wales and a special hello to the Miners of South Wales at this great festival. It is a great privilege to be participating in this historic festival and all the best to you as we strive towards a world where we all can live abundant, peaceful and dignified lives. I'm going to begin with one of my own songs, 'Didn't my Lord deliver Daniel, bringing freedom to our people'.

Film ends.

> *Didn't my Lord deliver Daniel, deliver Daniel, deliver Daniel,*
> *Didn't my Lord deliver Daniel, and why not every man?*
> *He delivered Daniel from the Lions den,*
> *Jonah from the belly of a whale,*

And the Hebrew Children from the fiery furnace and why not
                                                every man.
Didn't my Lord deliver Daniel, deliver Daniel, deliver Daniel,
Didn't my Lord deliver Daniel, and why not every man?
The moon runs down in a purple stream
The sun refused to shine
Every star did disappear
Yes freedom shall be mine.
Didn't My Lord deliver Daniel, deliver Daniel, deliver Daniel,
Didn't my Lord deliver Daniel, and why not every man?

During the song, GETHYN gets up on his chair.

SANDRA: Gethyn, sit down.

GETHYN (*as boy*): No.

SANDRA: Sit down.

GETHYN (*as boy*): No, I'm trying to see him.

SANDRA: You can't see him.

GETHYN (*as boy*): No, he's here somewhere.

SANDRA: He's in America.

GETHYN (*as boy*): No I wrote to him, see?

SANDRA (*to an imaginary member of the audience, behind GETHYN*): I'm sorry about this. (*Then to GETHYN:*) Geth!

GETHYN (*as boy*): Leave me.

SANDRA: Get down.

GETHYN (*as boy*): No, he's got to see me.

SANDRA grabs GETHYN and takes him out of the seating.

SANDRA (*to imaginary audience member*): Excuse me. Gethyn, come here. If you can't sit down, you'll have to stand, now ssh!

GETHYN starts to sing along.

SANDRA: Ssh!

GETHYN (*as boy*): You said I could sing with Paul Robeson.

SANDRA: Sing quietly then, people want to hear Paul.

GETHYN tries to sing quietly but gradually gets louder. SANDRA can't bring herself to stop him. He sings at the top of his voice. SANDRA tries not to laugh. Robeson stops singing.

WILL PAYNTER: Thank you very much, Paul. You know that the fervour with which we sing is no greater than the fervour with which we struggle in the cause of freedom for all peoples. And now I'm going to ask the Male Voice Choir and all this great audience to sing a song and to dedicate it to you, 'We'll keep a Welcome in the Hillside'.

The Porthcawl audience begin to sing. GETHYN speaks over the song.

GETHYN: Then I saw him, coming through the crowd. He'd spotted me standing on the chair. I knew if I wrote that he'd come. He'd not be able to resist.

GEORGE approaches, as GETHYN continues.

GETHYN: Somehow, in the midst of this precious communication, nothing less could have happened. We could hear in Robeson's voice the price he had paid, the toll that had been taken by those who would silence us. How could any of us feel afraid in our lives when he shamed us with his courage.

SANDRA sees GEORGE. He takes a flower from his lapel and puts it in her hair. They kiss at the climax to the song.

GETHYN: See, I knew Paul Robeson wouldn't let me down.

ROBESON: Until we meet!

GETHYN: Until we meet.

WILL PAYNTER: Thank you very much Paul and our best wishes to you.

ROBESON: Thanks again.

GETHYN: That night we travelled back up the valley on the train. Me, Mam and George. In the carriages, people were sharing the last of their food and drink. There were no differences any more, we had all been elevated, raised up over Jordan, and by the fact that we felt especially touched by this great man. 'Sing, sing!' They was shouting. Everyone had their turn. Then it came to us.

SANDRA (*nervous*): There is a song I want to sing. (*She whispers to GEORGE and GETHYN.*)

GETHYN: The carriage fell silent, bottoms nestled down for comfort and babies were held on laps, I wasn't sure if any sound would come out.

SANDRA begins singing. The others join her. She grows in confidence.

SANDRA: Sometimes I feel like a motherless child,
Sometimes I feel like a motherless child,
Sometimes I feel like a motherless child,
A long ways from home,
A long ways from home.
Come my brother, a longs ways from home, a long
ways from home.
Sometimes I feel like I'm almost gone,
Sometimes I feel like I'm almost gone,
Sometimes I feel like I'm almost gone,
A long ways from home,
A long ways from home.
Come my brother, a long ways from home,
A long ways from home.

GEORGE takes his cue and sings 'The Canoe Song'. The others join him.

GEORGE: I ee ico Ye-ged-air
I ee ico Ye-ged-air
The current swings, the water sings, a river
rhyme.
For light is the burden of labour
When each bends his back with his neighbour
So peace for all,
We stand or fall,
And all for each,
Until we reach
The journey's end.

THEY SING: I ee oco, I ee oco, I ee oco.
I ee oco, I ee oco, I ee oco.

GETHYN (*speaking over the singing*): By standing up in the midst of all these people, George had somehow become invisible, 'Who's that man with the lovely voice?' asked Mrs Big Glyn with the whole carriage listening? 'That's my Da,' says I, 'I've found him. That's my Da'.

THEY SING: Standing-a-strong, standing-a-wise,
Righter of wrong, hater of lies,
Laughed as he fought, worked as he played,
As he has taught, let it be made.
Away you go Ye-ged-air,
And make it so Ye-ged-air,
Together all the paddles fall in tune and time,
So look alive Ye-ged-air,
And dip and drive Ye-ged-air,
The current swings, the water sings, a river
rhyme.
For light is the burden of labour
When each bends his back with his neighbour
So peace for all,
We stand or fall,
And all for each,
Until we reach,
The journey's end.

Lights change.

Projection: A clip from 'The Proud Valley'. Robeson, Dick Parry and a group of miners are going on shift, down the pit.

DICK: Come on David give them a lead.

Robeson begins singing.

ROBESON: *Back to work and no reclining*
All through the night
Overhead the stars are shining
All through the night.

As the miners disappear in to the darkness, GETHYN waves them goodbye.

GETHYN: Goodbye Paul – and thanks for everything.

Lights fade.

The End.

Melissa Vincent, Declan Wilson and Mark Howell East
photograph by Joy Griffiths

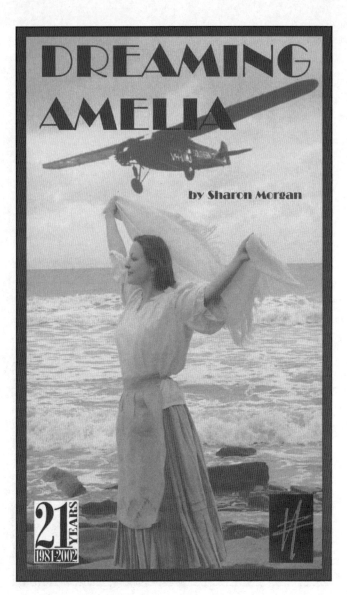

DREAMING
AMELIA

by Sharon Morgan

21 YEARS
1981-2002

Dreaming Amelia

Sharon Morgan

Dreaming Amelia was first performed at the Drama Studio, Whitchurch High School, Cardiff on Tuesday 24th September 2002.

Cast:

Betty	–	Sian McDowell
Rose/Amelia Earhart	–	Jessica Sandry
Madame/Shirley/ Martha Graham	–	Kath Dimery
Danny/Brian/Lou	–	David Lyndon

Creative Team:

Director	–	Chris Morgan
Composer	–	Paula Gardiner
Designers	–	Sid Scott Alison Callaghan
Choreographer	–	June Campbell Davies
Lighting Designer	–	Ceri James
Stage Manager	–	Brenda Knight

ACT ONE
Scene One

Burry Port on the Loughour Estuary, Carmarthen, South Wales, 1928-32.

BETTY and her mother, ROSE, are folding sheets in the kitchen of DANNY's rickety, old, boarded-up pub. ROSE uses the sheet-folding to help tell the story.

ROSE: Once upon a time in the Land of Sheets, everything was pure, clean and white. The capital of the Land of Sheets was called the Sparkling City and there lived Princess Betty. She sat on a gleaming glass throne and wore a cloak of silver satin trimmed with fluffy goose feathers. On her head was a shining tiara studded with diamonds and her feet were encased in slippers made of the softest white velvet tied with white satin bows.

One day Betty heard a noise – it was the silver bells of Sparkling City chiming to herald the arrival of a stranger. In her heart, she knew it would be a prince. She had been waiting so long. At last he rode up the palace path on his shining white stallion. 'Will you marry me?' he said to Princess Betty. 'Yes,' she said.

BETTY: But only if you dance with me first, without stepping on my toes.

ROSE and BETTY dance. BETTY tries to get ROSE to step on her toes.

ROSE: And he did so, and they got married...

BETTY: Step on my toes, step on my toes.

ROSE: And they lived happily ever after and they ruled the kingdom together.

BETTY: Step on my toes, I want to rule the kingdom on my own. Betty the proud! Betty the brave! Queen Betty.

ROSE: Sparkling Betty.

BETTY: Queen Betty. Why did you call me Betty, mam?

ROSE: After your grandmother.

BETTY: Why didn't you call me something romantic, like Sabrina, Arabella, or Dolly? (*She sings and dances, twirling the sheets.*) 'Goodbye Dolly, I must leave you...'

ROSE (*joins in the singing*): 'Though it breaks my heart to go. La La La...'

Enter DANNY. BETTY and ROSE immediately quiet and hurry to finish folding the sheets. DANNY is drunk and is carrying a half-empty bottle of whisky.

DANNY: I have just observed the senseless adulation...

BETTY: Big words – must be drunk.

ROSE: Ssh!

DANNY: Of the ludicrous.

ROSE: Food won't be long.

DANNY: A spectacle.

ROSE: Put the ironing things away, Betty.

DANNY: Only attractive...

ROSE takes the sheets off the chair and gives them to BETTY.

ROSE: Come and sit down Danny.

DANNY: To the mentally deficient.

DANNY sits down. ROSE kneels to take off his shoes.

ROSE: Fold them, Betty.

DANNY: I have been visiting the harbour... (*He swigs from the bottle.*)

ROSE: Glass!

BETTY goes to fetch a glass.

DANNY: Where thousands of ignorant fools have congregated.

BETTY is standing, fascinated, holding the glass.

ROSE: Betty!

BETTY brings the glass and DANNY pours whisky into it.

DANNY: They have come from afar with notebooks and cameras.

BETTY: People from the newspapers?

ROSE: Has there been an accident?

DANNY: You might call it that.

ROSE: A fishing boat?

DANNY: An aeroplane.

BETTY: An aeroplane!

DANNY: A seaplane to be accurate...

BETTY: A seaplane!

DANNY: Has landed in the estuary.

BETTY: I want to see.

DANNY: A seaplane laughingly called 'The Friendship'.

ROSE: Where did it come from?

DANNY: America.

BETTY: That's miles away.

DANNY: The sheriff Mr Fisher rowed out to greet it.

ROSE: Mr Fisher!

DANNY: And the unthinkable emerged.

BETTY: What! What?

DANNY: A woman.

BETTY: A woman in an aeroplane!

DANNY: She had somehow got it into her tiny little head that flying across the Atlantic...

BETTY: That's what I heard, like a bee only louder. I thought it was an eagle, gold and orange, a golden eagle flying in the sky! (*She dances wildly across the room.*)

DANNY: That flying across the Atlantic was a suitable pastime for a woman.

BETTY: It's historical!

ROSE: Hysterical more like. Put the ironing things away, Betty.

DANNY: It's unnatural.

BETTY: Burry Port's on the map!

DANNY: They grab at her garments as if she was the Messiah.

BETTY: We'll be in the paper.

DANNY: Deluded fools.

BETTY: Let's go down there, Mam.

ROSE: No need. Don't go. Not to go's the best thing. It doesn't matter to us.

DANNY: Don't go.

BETTY: I want to see.

DANNY: Don't go.

BETTY: Why not?

ROSE: 'Cos Danny said so.

BETTY: The whole village must be there.

DANNY: I said fools...

ROSE: They'll all be gone tomorrow. It'll all be back to normal tomorrow. (*She puts on Danny's slippers.*)

BETTY: Not for the woman. She'll be famous.

ROSE: Betty, go and get some firewood.

DANNY: The fools'll parade her.

BETTY: But she's done something special...

DANNY: There'll be flowers and brass bands.

BETTY: Something no woman's ever done.

DANNY: And what did I get? I fought a war and what did I get?

BETTY (*picks up two irons, lifts them above her head and marches around the room, chanting*): She's brave, she's strong, she's powerful.

DANNY leaps from the chair and grabs BETTY.

ROSE: Danny!

DANNY (*shouting*): I'll show you brave, I'll show you strong. She's a fool, d'you hear me? She's a freak, a sensation-seeker. She should be in the circus I said.

BETTY wriggles free and runs out.

ROSE: Betty!

ROSE stands, DANNY shakes.

DANNY: What did I get? Answer me, answer me, damn you!

ROSE: Nothing, Danny, nothing.

DANNY: Nothing, Rosie. I got nothing. (*He breaks down.*) Hold me, Rosie.

ROSE holds DANNY. She is stoic.

ROSE: It's all right Danny, it's alright.

Scene Two

The beach, adjacent to the pub.

BETTY's sharp exit, full of fear, turns into a dance which expresses her need to rise above her fear, humiliation and despair. Gradually, the dance becomes softer, more wistful. During the last third of the dance, a figure emerges on a higher lever and stands motionless, watching. It is AMELIA EARHART in her flying suit. BETTY ends her dance.

AMELIA (*clapping and cheering*): Bravo! Bravo!

BETTY is frightened and retreats to the far end of the beach.

AMELIA: I'm sorry. I didn't mean to frighten you. I probably am quite frightening; did you think I was a ghost? I sure do feel like some horrible creature from outer space. Please carry on – you have a gift, you have a future. I've never seen anyone dance so beautifully.

BETTY: You've probably never seen anyone dance at all – Man in the Moon!

AMELIA: Woman – oh yes, I am a woman! (*She takes off her flying hat.*) These are my flying clothes.

BETTY: You can fly! Like a bird in the sky?

AMELIA: Yes.

BETTY (*realising who she is talking to*): Got to go. I'm on a message.

AMELIA: Don't mind me. I was just passing.

BETTY: Never talk to strangers, my mother said.

AMELIA: Be careful. The harbour's rather crowded.

BETTY: Yes, d'you know why? A woman has just flown across the Atlantic.

AMELIA: Really? D'you know her name?

BETTY: No. Do you?

AMELIA: Yes I do.

106

BETTY: What is it?

AMELIA: Amelia Earhart. Pleased to meet you.

AMELIA proffers her hand. They shakes hands.

BETTY: Betty Parry, better go.

AMELIA: Stay with me Betty 'til the crowds have gone. They push and pull me 'til I don't know where I am. Where am I by the way?

BETTY: You're in Burry Port on the Loughour Estuary. Burry Port, Carmarthenshire, Wales, Great Britain, Europe, the World, the Universe.

AMELIA: Burry Port.

BETTY: 'Port of the Dunes' I call it.

AMELIA: The faraway land I thought I'd never get to.

BETTY: How can you start if you don't know where you'll finish?

AMELIA: I knew I was bound for somewhere. I had a vague idea that flying two thousand miles to the east over unbroken ocean would get me somewhere.

BETTY: Two thousand miles?

AMELIA: When you're offered a grand adventure you just don't refuse.

BETTY: A grand adventure?

107

AMELIA: A shining adventure.

BETTY: Weren't you afraid?

AMELIA: I had courage in my pocket. Courage and a silk bandana. (*She takes a crumpled piece of paper from her pocket.*)

BETTY: What's that?

AMELIA: Oh, it's just a poem I wrote.

BETTY: A poem?

AMELIA: D'you want to hear it?

BETTY nods.

AMELIA: OK. (*She reads:*)

> Courage is the price that life exacts for granting
> peace,
> the soul that knows it not knows no release from little
> things,
> knows not the livid loneliness of fear, nor mountain
> heights,
> where bitter joy can hear the sound of wings.
>
> How can Life grant us boon of living,
> compensate for dull grey ugliness and pregnant hate,
> Unless we dare
> The soul's dominion?
> Each time we make a choice we pay
> with courage to behold the restless day
> and count it fair.

I've been where no woman has gone, I have done what no woman's done. I have seen...

The lights change. AMELIA is surrounded by otherworldly light. Her bandana flutters in the breeze. BETTY kneels and adores.

AMELIA: A true rainbow, a circle of seven colours like the colour circle of Hawaii. I have been mesmerised by the vast and lovely glory of the sky. I have drunk its beauty in great gulps. I have seen the North Star on the wing tip. I have flown through mountains of clouds that reared their heads like dragons and dinosaurs and magical mythical monsters roaring at the sun. I have flown through golden valleys and over iridescent lakes over blue islands in pearly seas over secret forests and hidden continents and there were no horizons.

BETTY gets up, slowly, and starts to dance.

AMELIA: I leave the sorrows of the world behind, loss and shame and misery and false hopes. I fly above all sorrows, even the small sorrow of the rain. I am selfishly triumphant, I am ecstatic. I am escaping.

AMELIA stops and watches BETTY dance.

BETTY: That's how I feel when I dance. When I dance I fly like you, I leave the earth, I know nothing but my own pleasure. I am no longer me. I'm strong I'm brave I'm powerful I rule the world.

When BETTY turns around, AMELIA is gone. As BETTY runs to look for her, she notices, on the floor, the silk bandana and crumpled poem, 'Courage'. She picks them up and runs into the pub.

Scene Three

The pub.

ROSE is folding sheets. BETTY runs in.

BETTY: Mam! Mam!

ROSE: Ssh, be quiet, Danny's sleeping.

BETTY: He can sleep 'til kingdom come. You'll never guess who I've seen.

ROSE: Who?

BETTY: Guess! Guess!

ROSE: I don't know.

BETTY: Go on.

ROSE: Father Christmas.

BETTY: Amelia Earhart.

ROSE: Who?

BETTY: The woman who flew over the Atlantic.

ROSE: You went down to the harbour?

BETTY: I saw her on the beach. She said I was a lovely dancer. She talked to me. She's beautiful, she's tall and slim with sharp blue eyes and bobbed curly hair.

110

ROSE: You did, you went.

BETTY: She told me she'd seen pictures in the clouds.

ROSE: I know it's hard.

BETTY: Lands and animals.

ROSE: I do my best.

BETTY: Beautiful things. I do that when I lie on the beach.

ROSE: What we've got is all there is.

BETTY: But up there must be better.

ROSE: Dreams.

BETTY: You don't believe me, do you?

ROSE: If you dream too much it's bad for you.

BETTY: What about the Land of Sheets?

ROSE: That's just a story.

BETTY: I saw Amelia Earhart. On the beach.

ROSE: Dreams will drive you mad.

BETTY: I'm not mad and I'm not dreaming; I'm wide awake, you must believe me. I saw Amelia Earhart, I shook her hand and I've got proof.

BETTY shows ROSE the bandana and poem.

ROSE: The tide washed them in.

BETTY: No, it's writing, look, it's poetry.

ROSE: Did you take them?

BETTY: No, she gave them to me.

ROSE: If Danny finds out.

BETTY: Danny doesn't matter any more. Amelia Earhart said I could dance. I'm going to find a teacher. I'll be famous, Amelia said so, she said I had a gift. Dance with me, Mam. I'm so happy. I'll be a famous dancer and I'll take care of you. And we'll live in a big house and eat peaches and cream and wear flouncy chiffon dresses.

ROSE: Where did you come from?

BETTY: Dance, Mam. Dance.

ROSE: I can't, my lovely girl, I can hardly hold my back up. You dance, my sparkler, my sparkling Betty.

BETTY dances as the light fades.

Scene Four

The beach, two months later.

BRIAN: Hoi, Betty.

BETTY is far away.

112

BRIAN: Betty Parry!

BETTY turns to look.

BRIAN: I've got a parcel for you from America.

BETTY: Very funny.

BRIAN: I have, look.

BETTY: How d'you know it's for me?

BRIAN: It's my job, in the Post Office. I know every letter, every card, every parcel and who it's for. I know where everybody lives and I know who you are Betty Parry and I know this is a parcel for you from America.

BETTY: There's no parcel for me from America.

BRIAN: It's got to be for you.

BETTY: Nothing's got to be.

BRIAN: Yes it has.

BETTY: It's not for me.

BRIAN: Yes it is, it's got your name on. Look.

BETTY (*looks hurriedly, then looks away, hiding the fact she cannot read*): Where?

BRIAN: There.

BETTY: Oh, yes. Who's it from then?

BRIAN: Amelia Earhart.

BETTY: Liar.

BRIAN: Cross my heart.

BETTY: See the green.

BRIAN: People are usually pleased when they get parcels.

BETTY: What's the address?

BRIAN: Didn't you see it's for the Post Office?

BETTY: It's not another Betty Parry then?

BRIAN: There is no other Betty Parry. You're the one and only.

BETTY: Maybe it should've gone to Llanelli. Maybe it's lost.

BRIAN: Our procedures are impeccable. Sometimes parcels do get lost, but it's very rare.

BETTY: Who did you say it was from?

BRIAN: Amelia Earhart. The woman who flew the Atlantic. She was here two months ago. You've got a short memory. Here look: Amelia Earhart, New York. It could be money. She sent it registered. Are you related?

BETTY: Could be.

BRIAN: I'm sure it's money. You've got to sign.

BETTY: Can I open it?

BRIAN: If you sign. Because it's registered. There's a pen.

BETTY: I can't.

BRIAN: Go on.

BETTY: No, I can't.

BRIAN: Why not?

BETTY (*turns away, ashamed*): Doesn't matter. Send it back.

BRIAN: You don't have to write all your name, just B and P'll do. (*Pause.*) I'll do it if you like. Nobody'll know.

BETTY: Go on then.

BRIAN signs. Betty opens the parcel with great wonderment.

BETTY: It is money. It's for my dancing lessons. Now I can be who I want.

BRIAN: What's wrong with being you?

BETTY: Then I can go away.

BRIAN: What's wrong with here?

BETTY: You've got to go away to be rich and famous.

BRIAN: The grass is always greener.

BETTY: I'll have to find a teacher.

BRIAN: I wanted to be a teacher once.

BETTY: Why didn't you?

BRIAN: The war came.

BETTY: So?

BRIAN: Never mind. I'll teach you if you like.

BETTY: To dance?

BRIAN: To read and write. I won't tell anyone.

BETTY: What?

BRIAN: That you can't.

BETTY: There's no one to tell. Everybody knows.

BRIAN: Why haven't we met before?

BETTY: We have.

BRIAN: You're not the same.

BETTY: I am sparkling Betty of the Land of Sheets. Don't tell me, you're the Silver Prince.

BRIAN: Brian Jones of the Post Office. Look there's a letter.

BETTY: Read it to me then.

BRIAN begins to read the letter from Amelia. After the first sentence, we hear AMELIA's voice and then, slowly, out of the ether, AMELIA materialises, as in Scene Two's flying speech.

116

BRIAN (*reading*): Dear Betty, what an incredible welcome! Home Sweet Home...

AMELIA (*taking over*): Played by the New York Fire Department, streams of water shooting into the air, whistles blowing, a crowd of five hundred. Then up Broadway in a blizzard of ticker tape. Riding up Main Street while people throw telephone books at you is an amusing modern version of the triumphal march. Received the key to the city of New York from acting Mayor Joseph McKee and we auctioned a flag from the Friendship, and Charles Winniger, star of Showboat beat Babe Ruth to it at $650. Then on to Boston and flowers, flowers everywhere. I was presented with a blue Roadster and went shopping for hats – then Pennsylvania, Chicago, Toledo, Pittsburgh. There is no rest, no privacy. A short while ago I was earning $35 a week as a social worker and no one knew who I was, life will never be the same again.

To whom it may concern: this young lady... (*her voice continues, as the lights cross fade into the next scene.*)

Scene Five

Madame's studio.

Plink-plonk of ballet class piano music. MADAME is in the middle of a class. BETTY enters, shyly, the bandana in her hand.

AMELIA (*continuing*): Has the most mysterious ability to communicate with her body. Please develop this, giving her discipline and focus without dampening her innate energy and spirit.

MADAME: And point and close, and point and close. Good, and *plies bon bon c'est tres bon*. Come in, come in, never mind if you are late. Come in and join in as best you can.

BETTY stands in shock.

MADAME: And don't forget the arms. Heads up, eyes forward, concentrate.

MADAME, as she speaks, moves towards BETTY.

MADAME: And *grand battements*, and lift, and point and...

BETTY: Are you a dancer?

MADAME: Am I a dancer? In the morning, in the night, with no shame on summer afternoons I dance... and *developés* and one... where are your shoes? Have you forgotten them? Never mind, we have some here. Try these.

BETTY sits to put on the shoes. MADAME helps her tie the ribbons.

BETTY: Are you foreign?

MADAME: Madame Irina. Trained at the Maryinksi.

BETTY: Where's that?

MADAME: Saint Petersburg, Russia. Before the Revolution.

BETTY: What's a revolution?

MADAME: When everything changes so much it's no longer recognisable.

BETTY: That sounds like me.

MADAME: When the world's turned upside down.

BETTY: I'm going to be somebody new.

MADAME: But dancing stays the same. I have danced with Diaghilev. I have danced with Pavlova.

BETTY: I ought to change my name.

MADAME (*in a world of her own, she dances*): I have danced the Dying Swan, Giselle. I have danced the Firebird in crimson sequins and golden feathers, and when I was in Paris I wore mink coats and silver shoes.

BETTY (*watching, entranced*): Are you famous?

MADAME: Of course. And rich. Now, you.

BETTY: I can't dance here.

MADAME: *Pour quois pas?* Why not?

BETTY: I don't know the room. It's strange to me.

MADAME: Dancers dance in many strange rooms, that's where we practice and repeat like this. (*She repeats a* pas de chat *four times, quickly.*)

BETTY: I can't do that. I don't do that. I don't dance like that.

MADAME: Then how do you dance?

BETTY stands, paralysed.

MADAME: Who is this Amelia Earhart?

BETTY: She flew across the Atlantic.

MADAME: She has wings?

BETTY: She's an angel.

MADAME: And did she fly so near the sun she was struck blind? Show me. What did she see? A mirage? Was her mind playing tricks with her? Are you playing tricks with me?

BETTY: No, Madame.

MADAME: Show me, then. Dance!

BETTY begins to dance, angrily.

MADAME: See, you can dance in a strange room.

BETTY (*stops dancing – mid-flow, ecstatic*): You'll teach me then. I can pay you.

MADAME: You know nothing and you know everything. Let's begin at the beginning, hand on the barre.

BETTY holds on to the barre, doing exercises. MADAME speaks and the whole sequence develops into a triumphant dance.

MADAME: Do you go to school?

BETTY: I work with my mother. She's a washer woman.

MADAME: Like Pavlova, Anna Pavlova. And your father's dead?

BETTY: How did you know.

MADAME: And *pliés* and bend and...

BETTY: Don't tell anyone, no one must know.

MADAME: Eh *bien*, it will be our little secret, but you must promise to work hard, back straight, knees taut, head up, every part of you, every little piece of you must be under control, under the control of this (*she taps her forehead*), this is the beginning and the end.

We do not move on a whim, anyhow, because today we feel like doing so but tomorrow we may not. And turn and arabesques, good, drop that shoulder.

BETTY is now out on the floor.

MADAME: It will take days, weeks, months, years of practice, repeating the same thing over and over. You are not just bored with it, merely tired of the movement. You hate yourself that you cannot get it exactly right. You do it in your sleep, you hate the movement, there is no half measure, no in-between; the head exactly here, the neck exactly there – over and over again 'til you believe you'll never do it, that it's no good however hard you try it will not work. The machine will not work because your body is like a machine. You press this button it does this, you press the other is does that, it must respond *immediatement* as if to an alarm call, an emergency. And then after a long, long time, eventually after centuries of toil it will become an instrument that you will play and you will play so many tunes, happy tunes, funny tunes. You will express pain and laughter, hope and defeat. It is in your body but it starts in the head. If your head is strong you control your whole being, then you will be strong, nobody can hurt you. You will become invulnerable.

Two years have passed. The dance ends triumphantly. BETTY, now sixteen, crosses to put her shoes in her bag. She puts on her dress, takes out the crumpled poem from her pocket and reads it fluently.

BETTY: Courage is the price that life exacts for granting peace. The soul that knows it not knows no release from little things.

Scene Six

The beach, 1930.

Lights have cross faded. BETTY has reached the beach. As she walks towards the pub, she reads the letter from Amelia and AMELIA appears.

BETTY: Dear Betty, I have met all my goals, fulfilled all my contracts, kept all my promises.

AMELIA: Ida Tarbell – a well-known journalist – has named me as one of the fifty living women who have done the most for the United States. Can you imagine! She said I showed ability to 'initiate and create, lead and inspire'.

BETTY and AMELIA: Wow!

AMELIA: As usual, I have been writing reams for Cosmopolitan, and Aero News and Mechanics. As you know I have been elected President of the ninety-niners, and we are busy as ever supporting women aviators. I was so pleased to hear of the unveiling of the commemorative column in Burry Port. I may see you sooner than you think. I'm planning to cross the Atlantic again. I've broken three world speed records...

BETTY and AMELIA: But I fancy doing something big.

BETTY is exhilarated and runs towards the pub.

Scene Seven

The pub.

DANNY is sitting in his chair, drunk. He has deteriorated. BETTY enters and tries to go upstairs without being seen.

DANNY: Where've you been, Betty?

BETTY freezes.

DANNY: Come here so I can see you. Come here!

BETTY goes and stands some way away.

DANNY: You're different, Betty. You've changed. You're out a lot. Where d'you go, Betty? That a new dress? Where d'you get that, then?

ROSE enters, carrying washing.

DANNY: Rosie, Rosie, come here. Look at her. She doesn't look the same. What d'you think, Rosie?

ROSE: She's growing, Danny. She's sixteen. She's a young lady now.

DANNY: Lady is it? Got a fancy man have you, to pay for it?

BETTY moves to go.

DANNY: I'm talking to you! Where did you get that dress? I've seen you with the fishermen.

BETTY and ROSE speak simultaneously.

BETTY: I got it second-hand.

ROSE: I made it from an old frock of mine.

DANNY: Funny. I somehow don't recall that particular combination of colours and shapes.

BETTY: Mam had lots of dresses when we came here first.

DANNY: So who is truthful and who is the liar? Where've you been Betty, where've you been in your smart new dress? Have you been worshipping at the shrine? The shrine to that funny woman, the freak, the fool, the circus act.

BETTY moves to go.

DANNY: No, stay. I've got something to show you. (*He produces newspaper cuttings of Amelia, which Betty has been keeping.*) Look, Rosie. Newspapers. Stories about that funny woman.

BETTY: Give me those.

BETTY grabs at them but DANNY keeps them out of her reach.

DANNY: What d'you want these for? You can't read.

BETTY: You took me out of school.

ROSE: She could have been top of the class. I told him, Betty.

DANNY: Your mother needed help.

BETTY: Why don't you work, Danny?

DANNY: I fought a war.

BETTY: All you do is sit and drink.

DANNY: And who are you then? Little Miss Nobody no point in schooling you. You're stupid.

BETTY (*drops her bag, grabs a newspaper and beings to read*): 'Today the FAI registered three world speed records in the name of Amelia Earhart.'

ROSE: Betty!

BETTY: 'Miss Earhart, the darling of America.'

DANNY: What's in this bag?

BETTY: Nothing.

DANNY: D'you hear that, Rosie? Betty carries a bag of nothingness around with her, to match the nothing in her head. Let's see this nothingness. Well, well, curiouser and curiouser. (*He takes out her ballet shoes, tights, etc.*) What have we here then? What does Betty want with dancing shoes?

BETTY: To dance with. I'm having dancing lessons.

ROSE: It's just a hobby, Danny.

DANNY: No wonder you don't pull your weight. Who's paying then?

ROSE: I am.

BETTY: Amelia Earhart.

DANNY: Watch your tongue.

ROSE: I'm paying Danny.

DANNY: What was that? Did my ears deceive me? Rose is paying. Rose the rich, Rose the millionaire. Have you been seeing the fishermen too? They don't pay very well do they? Rose, now answer me. Can you afford to pay for dancing lessons and dancing shoes and frocks and newspapers. Can you?

ROSE says nothing.

DANNY: Can you?

DANNY grabs ROSE.

DANNY: Damn you, answer me! Can you?

ROSE: No.

DANNY: Louder

ROSE: No!

DANNY: Did you hear that, Betty? We can't afford it. Your mother doesn't earn enough. So you won't be needing these anymore. (*He grabs a scissors and begins to cut up the shoes and clothes.*)

BETTY launches herself at DANNY.

DANNY: Earning paltry sums and squandering it on frivolities.

BETTY: Leave them alone, they're mine, give them to me. (*She cuts herself, on the scissors.*)

DANNY: And that's where you're wrong little nobody, they're mine. I'm your legal guardian. What's yours is mine. You are mine, everything in this bag is mine. (*He turns the bag upside down – notes and coins fall out.*) What generous fishermen. You must have put your prices up. Take two of you to earn this much in a year. Where did this come from?

ROSE goes to speak, but BETTY pre-empts her.

BETTY: Amelia Earhart sends it to me.

DANNY: Registered charity are we?

BETTY: It's for dancing lessons.

DANNY: You've never met her, liar.

BETTY: Because I'm talented.

DANNY: No doubt she sends it regularly.

BETTY: She's been sending it for months. (*She picks up the money.*)

DANNY: That's nice. I need money on a regular basis.

BETTY: She sends it to the post office. You ask Brian.

DANNY: Let's get this straight. Amelia Earhart sends money to you for no reason at all.

BETTY: I'm going to be famous.

DANNY: I need some money.

BETTY: To waste on whisky.

DANNY: It would be rather useful.

BETTY: To drink yourself to death.

DANNY: Now there's a thought.

BETTY (*stands up, having collected every note and coin*): I've got a gift.

DANNY: Now so have I. Give it to me. (He screams:) Give it to me.

ROSE: Give it to him Betty.

BETTY gives DANNY the money. DANNY lurches out. BETTY cries.

ROSE: It's the drink.

BETTY: Last time it was the war.

ROSE: It's the war that makes him drink.

BETTY Well it's not my fault. I didn't start the bloody war.

ROSE: Don't swear, Betty.

BETTY (*shouting as she runs off*): Don't swear, Betty. Don't dance, Betty. Don't, don't, don't, don't be you, Betty. What's the point in living.

Scene Eight

The beach, two months later.

BRIAN: Betty! Betty Parry! The one and only. (*He approaches.*) You're quiet these days.

BETTY doesn't answer.

BRIAN: Busy?

BETTY still doesn't answer. BRIAN sees the poem and bandana.

BRIAN: I think you should know that off by heart by now, I do. Amelia's doing wonderful things, still daring the soul's dominion. I heard it on the radio. You should get a radio, Betty. Marvellous invention. But then, you know all about it from the letters. Flying to Honolulu. Flying over the gulf of Mexico, landing in a dry lake bed. And of course, getting married. She's got two canaries now, and she's wanted one forever.

BETTY tries hard to not react.

BRIAN: Has she mentioned an Atlantic crossing?

BETTY: Yes, yes.

BRIAN: Will you read them to me sometime? The newspapers only give you the bare facts. Read these to me, then.

BRIAN hands BETTY the newspapers. She hands them back.

BETTY: You can read, Brian, you read them.

BRIAN: I like to hear you. You read so well.

BETTY: Some other time.

Pause.

BRIAN: Don't see you getting the bus to Llanelli much.

BETTY: I don't do dancing now.

BRIAN: Your stepfather's getting out a lot. He's down the pub most every night.

BETTY: I don't do dancing and you can cancel my newspapers. Amelia Earhart gets along without me very well. I'm not interested in her anymore. I've got to go now. Mam needs help. I've got a lot of washing and ironing to do.

Scene Nine

The pub.

ROSE is ironing. BETTY enters and goes to pick up a sheet from a pile in the laundry basket.

BETTY: Help me fold this, Mam.

ROSE goes to her and they begin to fold the sheet, in silence.

ROSE: At least he's out.

BETTY: Yes.

ROSE: And then he'll fall asleep.

BETTY: Collapse.

Pause.

ROSE: Talk to Madame Irina.

BETTY: What for?

ROSE: Explain what's happened.

BETTY: What's happened, Mam?

ROSE: Write to Amelia.

BETTY What's happened? My stepfather's taken the money, I give him the parcels now? He takes the money and spends it all on drink! We're afraid of him.

131

ROSE: I've told you it's the war...

BETTY: That makes him drink and when he drinks: he calls – we run; he shouts – we jump.

ROSE: He can't help it.

BETTY: Does that make everything alright?

ROSE: I'm sorry.

BETTY: It's my life and you're sorry.

ROSE: He wasn't like that before...

BETTY: I don't care. All I wanted to do was dance. I was going somewhere.

ROSE: What d'you want to go for?

BETTY: I can't do anything, Mam. I feel as if I don't exist. I've got no strength to move or think. I'll never dance again.

ROSE: You'll always dance.

BETTY: I don't want to dance.

ROSE: You enjoy it.

BETTY: Dancing out the back.

ROSE: I enjoy it.

BETTY: I want to dance properly.

ROSE: It was beautiful.

BETTY: I knew nothing then. Now I've learnt so many things. Now I've seen what I can be, the secret's round the corner, but I can't get there.

ROSE: You want to see what's on the other side of the mountain.

BETTY: Yes.

ROSE: You don't need to do that.

BETTY: I must.

ROSE: You never did before.

BETTY: Before I met Amelia?

ROSE: Giving you ideas.

BETTY: You don't believe I can be someone.

ROSE: You are someone.

BETTY: Danny's right. I'm nobody.

ROSE: Clever, pretty.

BETTY: Ugly, stupid.

ROSE: You're strong.

BETTY: I'm weak.

133

ROSE: Brave. Brave Betty, sparkling Betty.

BETTY: Frightened Betty. I'm afraid, Mam. Amelia Earhart flew across the Atlantic. She is brave. She's on a grand adventure, a shining adventure. I was on a shining adventure too, but now I'm not. I'm afraid to move and so are you. There's nothing brave about living in a ramshackle, old, boarded-up pub, washing clothes all day for sixpence a time.

ROSE: You can't go on like this.

BETTY: Be quiet is it? Keep my head down.

ROSE: You've got your life in front of you. You're wasting time.

BETTY: Put up with it? Say nothing.

ROSE: You've got to face up to reality.

BETTY: I am, I am. I'll never dance again.

ROSE: You've got to get on with it.

BETTY: I will then. I'll dig a hole in the ground and cover myself with earth. And then I'll lie dark in the deep, not moving where no one can see me and I can see no one.

ROSE: Dance with me, Betty. My sparkler. Dance with me. Come on.

ROSE goes to BETTY – who is hunched up on the floor – and tries to pull her up, with no success.

ROSE: Come on. Stand up. Come on.

BETTY gets up, reluctantly, and stands stiffly.

ROSE: Now, if you put one foot in front of the other you'll find you'll move and you'll feel better. Come on, Betty. Dance.

BETTY: You dance, Mam, go on, you dance.

ROSE begins to dance, tiredly, stiffly. But we can see where Betty got her talent. ROSE talks as she moves, sings a childhood song.

ROSE: Do you remember how we used to laugh. In front of the fire after your bath.
    'After the ball is over la la la la la la
    And you had one curl on top of your head la la la la la...'

We haven't seen ROSE this happy, before now. She continues to dance. MADAME enters.

MADAME (*joining in the song*): La la la...

ROSE stops as she hears MADAME's voice.

BETTY: Mam, this is Madame Irina.

MADAME: *Enchanté.* So this is where the magic comes from.

ROSE: Sit down, please. Excuse the mess, we're in the middle of it, all this rain...

MADAME: Where have you been, Elizabeth? We have lots of work to do. This is very naughty.

BETTY: I don't want to dance anymore.

MADAME: I have exciting news for you, but first you must explain. What is it, you don't want to in a room?

BETTY: In a room, in a yard, on a beach, in a boat, on a mountain, in the moon, in the stars. I never want to dance again.

MADAME: Not even in a theatre? With red velvet curtains trimmed with golden braid with stalls and a circle and boxes for the rich. And dressing rooms and make-up and costumes.

ROSE: What is this?

MADAME: There is an opportunity for Betty to dance in a show, some solos. There will be a tour.

ROSE: Betty.

BETTY: I can't.

ROSE: You try...

ROSE leaves MADAME to persuade BETTY.

BETTY: I can't.

MADAME: You can.

BETTY: I can't, you can't understand.

MADAME: Why not?

BETTY: There's no money anymore. The money stopped.

MADAME: You won't have to pay to dance. They'll pay you.

BETTY: They'll pay me?! To dance?!

MADAME: Yes.

BETTY: They'll pay me for dancing?

MADAME: Yes. Not much at first. But it will be something.

BETTY: I can pay for lessons. Amelia won't need to send me money. I can write to her and tell her she won't need to send me money.

MADAME: See you in class tomorrow. Be prompt.

BETTY (*reading*): Dear Betty, you didn't write last time so I guess you must be busy or maybe it got lost in transit...

AMELIA (*appearing in the ghostly light*): I hope the dancing's going well. I will insist on finding out even if I have to fly the ocean to visit.

As Amelia speaks, BETTY puts on a chiffon ballet frock.

AMELIA: I'm planning an Atlantic crossing pretty soon. Maybe I'll get to see your first performance. Just think of me sitting in the theatre looking at you, watching you dance.

BETTY begins to dance.

AMELIA: I'll be one in a hundred, maybe thousands, maybe you won't know where I am, you'll just know I'm there somewhere watching you and marvelling, spellbound by the precision of your movements, your beauty your fragile elegance and the poetry of the emotion you express. (*She fades.*)

Scene Ten

BETTY continues to dance. She's on a stage. She takes a curtain call – there is applause. She loves it. MADAME stands in the wings and puts a shawl around BETTY's shoulders.

MADAME: Very good *ma petite*.

BETTY: They like me, I feel wonderful.

MADAME: You are on the top of the world.

BETTY: To do it for someone. To show it to someone.

MADAME: And know they like it.

BETTY: Yes. No sound, no movement – only mine. They were so still but I could feel them, all of them as one being, responding to me.

MADAME: When you were sad...

BETTY: They were sad. When I moved fast...

MADAME: They ran with you...

BETTY: They were inside me and I was inside them...

138

MADAME: Moving together...

BETTY: Yes! I took them by the hand and we went on a journey, to where no one's ever been before. We walked untrodden paths, we were in a mysterious place... and no one will ever go there again.

MADAME: It is a once-only opportunity, a once-only experience, and at the end, when we come down to earth again, and they applaud, it is for themselves as much as you because without them watching you couldn't go there. You need them as much as they need you.

BETTY: Now I've found them once, I've been there once, now I know this other world is there, I can go back. I must go back. I need to. For the first time ever I feel completely me.

MADAME: Ah *ma petite* you have discovered the power of performance. But don't get ideas – class tomorrow. Practice, practice, practice. It is a never-ending search for control. You mustn't let the instrument get rusty or it will not be a useful tool and then you will not be as one. Then you will lose your audience. Yes yes, you have discovered your public. Yes it's so exciting – and addictive.

Scene Eleven

The pub, 1932.

BETTY is eighteen. ROSE is ironing Betty's last costume for her tour. BETTY is packing the others into a suitcase.

ROSE: And where this week?

BETTY: Swansea, Brecon, Merthyr Tydfil and two others I can't remember. Treorchy, probably, or Ebbw Vale.

ROSE: You can't remember?

BETTY: The show's the same, the place is different.

ROSE: But it's a living. And you love the show.

BETTY: Same dances, same costumes.

ROSE: And you've a crowd.

BETTY: It was exciting to begin with.

ROSE: When it was new. But now?

BRIAN (*off-stage*): Betty, Betty, Betty Parry! The one and only. (*He enters.*) I've got something for you.

BETTY: What is it?

ROSE: Guess.

BETTY: Give it to me, Brian, it could be urgent.

BETTY wrestles the object from BRIAN.

BRIAN: It's a telegram.

ROSE: Bad news.

BRIAN: No, good news.

BETTY: How do you know?

BRIAN: I accepted it.

BETTY (*reading*): Flown across Atlantic STOP Landed in a field in Connemara STOP Can't come to Wales STOP Come to America STOP Amelia. (*She reacts:*) She wants me to come to America – America! To come to America!

ROSE: She doesn't mean it...

BETTY: I've got to go America. New York! It's the most exciting city in the world.

ROSE: You can't expect Amelia to...

BETTY: I'll save up, I'll work my passage, I'll dance my way over. There must be dancers on these big ships. Madame will know. She went there with Pavlova.

Silence.

BETTY: You don't want me to go do you, Mam?

ROSE: Is it safe?

BETTY: Is it safe here?

ROSE says nothing.

BETTY: Come with me, Mam.

ROSE: I can't do that, I have to...

BETTY: Take care of Danny.

ROSE: Yes, to stay and look after Danny. America, that's better than the Land of Sheets, and I'm sure the Silver Prince will come.

BETTY: I don't want a silver prince, I want to dance there and be famous.

ROSE: I can see your name in lights, sparkling Betty.

BETTY: I'll come back.

ROSE: I know you will.

BETTY: New York. I won't tell Amelia. Not to begin with, but as soon as my name's in lights I'll send her complimentary tickets for the best seats in the house.

BETTY picks up the dress Rose was ironing. She puts it on and begins to tap dance and sing. ROSE and BRIAN join in.

BETTY: Now come on and listen to the Lullaby of Broadway.

BETTY, ROSE and BRIAN: 'La la la la la la la the Lullaby of Broadway...'

Scene Twelve

America.

Amelia, Eleanor Roosevelt, Mae West and Clark Gable on film. BETTY, ROSE and BRIAN continue to dance and sing as the lights cross fade. They are replaced by images of Amelia in America and Betty on the moonlit deck of a steamship, seeing these images in the clouds.

NEWSCASTER'S VOICE: Last night our first lady took a night-time flight over Baltimore and Washington, with her friend Amelia Earhart. Both ladies, dressed in evening gowns, saw the lights of the capital city, courtesy of Eastern Airlines.

Cross fade to:

NEWSCASTER'S VOICE: Amelia Earhart designs and models her collection of simple but beautifully-cut dresses, suits and separates for American Vogue. Who could imagine a more charming model.

Cross fade to:

NEWSCASTER'S VOICE: In Hollywood today a star of the sky meets the stars of the silver screen. Amelia Earhart posed for these photographers with Mae West and Clark Gable at Universal Studios. Shall we be seeing our favourite Aviatrix on celluloid soon?

Scene Thirteen

New York, America, 1933-34.

BETTY is auditioning for a part in a Broadway show. She is dancing badly; not smiling, stumbling. Amelia's bandana is around her neck. The dance is 'Lullaby of Broadway'. Her mutterings becomes louder. In the end, she sings them and they become the lyrics.

BETTY: Come along and watch me dance, this is my moment, please, please give me one more chance to show you I can do it. If I can't do this right then I'm not a dancer,

143

what about the opening night? I don't have an answer. I'm not usually like this, usually I enjoy it, I've worked damn hard on this, why can't I do it? If I get rejection one more time, it'll be the last time, I can't face it once again, this'll be the last time.

The music stops. Silence. BETTY shades her eyes to look into the auditorium.

BETTY: Sorry? What? Yes... thank you. I'm sorry. Thank you. (*She gathers up her bag and rushes off stage. In the wings, she dances and sings defiantly again, to the same tune.*) New York City's a big place, with lots of hungry dancers. I'm lost, alone in this rat race.

Oh! Just give me a chance. Dear Amelia, why can't I do it? In my room I'm a star, I'm perfection, when I step on the stage I go to pieces, I feel my power drain away. I think of Mam and the land of sheets but it only makes me feel sad. I think of Madame and I'm ten times worse. Every step, every word is ingrained in my bones and still my mind gives way. (*She takes Amelia's bandana off and holds it. She takes the poem from her pocket. She holds them both, her eyes tightly shut. She prays to Amelia.*) Please Amelia, make me brave, help me think of it as a grand adventure, help me do it for the fun of it, all I need is a bit of magic. Please Amelia, let them pick me for a show, any show for one small part, the chorus would do. If I could see you now, just for a little while, if I could hear your voice, to give me strength. (*She begins to dance, as she did in Act One.*)

AMELIA (*in her flying suit*): I leave the sorrows of the world behind me loss and misery.

BETTY joins in, as she dances.

BETTY: I leave the earth, I know nothing but the pleasure in movement. I am no longer me, I am strong, I am brave, I'm powerful, I rule the world.

AMELIA: And the false hopes. I am no longer sad. I feel the exhilaration of escape. I am selfishly triumphant. I have eluded care, I fly above all sorrows, even the small sorrow of the rain.

BETTY stops, as she sees AMELIA.

AMELIA: That was beautiful. You have a special talent, a mysterious quality, you are truly a natural dancer so just get out there and enjoy! Go do it for the fun of it, courage is the price....

BETTY continues, as AMELIA disappears.

BETTY: That life exacts. (*She begins to tap dance 'Lullaby of Broadway', as she quotes from the poem. She dances back into the spotlight.*) For granting peace, the soul that knows it not, knows no release from little things. (*She continues to dance – smilingly, totally confident. She puts on a glittery costume. She is now in a performance. She takes several curtain calls. Flowers are thrown.*)

ACT TWO
Scene One

Betty's dressing room in a big Broadway Theatre, 1934.

BETTY comes off stage, exhausted. SHIRLEY, sat at her dressing table, throws a a robe around BETTY. SHIRLEY removes her headgear. BETTY brushes her hair. BETTY now has an American accent.

SHIRLEY: Your first solo spot. That sure was something.

BETTY: Do you think so, Shirley?

SHIRLEY: Sure do. I thought those calls would never end. Oh, they love you alright.

BETTY: Do they?

SHIRLEY: You sparkle. You're a star. They can't take their eyes off you. I've seen it before.

BETTY: Have you really? Really, Shirley?

SHIRLEY: Believe me, when you come on they see nothing else.

BETTY: It's like a dream, Shirley.

SHIRLEY: It's no dream, this is real kid and you deserve it, you've worked hard. This is the start of something big. Just don't get carried away that's all.

LOU emerges from the shadows. He is a faded, handsome, charmer. BETTY is embarrassed. SHIRLEY's seen it all before.

146

LOU: Oh, let her Shirley, let her be transported on the magic carpet of her deepest desires to the mysterious lands few mortals dare explore.

BETTY stands. She is scantily dressed.

LOU: Don't be frightened. Lou Daniels – theatrical agent.

LOU hands BETTY his card. BETTY is impressed, SHIRLEY is not.

LOU: Beautiful, utterly beautiful!

LOU produces a bottle of champagne and hands it to SHIRLEY, without taking his eyes off BETTY.

LOU: A cause for celebration. Sit down, Betty.

BETTY sits, mesmerised. LOU sits opposite her.

LOU: Give me your foot.

BETTY does so, without taking her eyes off LOU.

LOU: Ah, what loveliness! That arch! Such pretty knees!

LOU unstraps BETTY's shoes.

LOU: I would drink from your satin, bejewelled slipper....

SHIRLEY (*putting two glasses on the table*): But I wouldn't let you – glasses.

LOU: And the other foot that is as magical as the first. These feet are capable of such trickery.

147

LOU unstraps BETTY's other shoe.

LOU: They would have us believe you are an angel, a fairy queen, some ethereal creature escaped from eternity.

BETTY is overwhelmed. She stands. So does LOU. He pours champagne into the glasses.

LOU: A toast. Join us Shirley, why don't you?

SHIRLEY: I got work to do, Lou Daniels.

LOU and BETTY clink glasses and drink. BETTY drinks much too much, much too fast. SHIRLEY holds up a dress.

SHIRLEY: Your dress.

BETTY: Thank you.

SHIRLEY hangs the dress behind the screen and stands waiting, watching, while LOU and BETTY look at each other.

SHIRLEY: It's waiting for you.

LOU: You'd better go and change.

BETTY: Yes. Excuse me.

LOU: Don't mind me.

BETTY goes behind the screen, flirting as she changes.

LOU: Beautiful legs, beautiful arms, beautiful everything. Shall we take New York by storm tonight?

BETTY: What did you have in mind?

LOU: Eating, drinking, being merry....

SHIRLEY: Said the spider to the fly.

BETTY: Oh, let's go to Caesar's!

LOU: Your wish is my command.

SHIRLEY: Heads will turn. Tongues will wag.

LOU: When I walk in with you on my arm...

SHIRLEY: They'll all say...

LOU: What a lucky man! Is he really Betty Parry's agent?

BETTY: You want to represent me?!

BETTY'S bra appears. SHIRLEY grabs it, quickly.

LOU: It would be an honour.

SHIRLEY: She'll have to think about it.

BETTY (*seductively*): Is that all? (*She drapes one stocking over the screen.*)

SHIRLEY: Of course it's not.

BETTY's other stocking is draped over the screen.

LOU: Of course it's not.

149

BETTY: What else do you want?

LOU: To share thrilling conversations. I'll listen to your stories, I'll tell you mine.

SHIRLEY: Wouldn't I love to be there.

BETTY's suspender belt appears. SHIRLEY whips it away.

BETTY: To buy me pretty things?

LOU: The prettiest! Boxes of candy and pink sugared almonds to put into your soft wet mouth.

BETTY: And chocolate truffles.

LOU: Musky perfumes.

BETTY: In coloured bottles.

BETTY emerges in her civvies. SHIRLEY brings BETTY her shoes.

LOU: Let me, let me. Sit down, princess.

SHIRLEY moves BETTY's chair forward.

LOU: Silk stockings.

BETTY: Lacy lingerie.

LOU: Feather boas.

BETTY: And satin gloves.

LOU: A velvet cape.

BETTY: With a fur-trimmed collar.

LOU and BETTY speak faster and faster. They stand. She wants LOU to kiss her. LOU wants to kiss her, but decides not to, so BETTY kisses him. She disappears, as LOU turns his back to the audience.

LOU: You'll have to change your name.

BETTY: Isabella, Anastasia, Who shall I be? Gloria!

BETTY runs away. Lou chases her.

Scene Two

Two mannequins are skating on a frozen lake. It is snowing. Coloured lights swirl over the stage, revealing shops selling glittering things and mannequins modelling glittery dresses.

LOU (*off-stage*): Bethany? Bethany!

LOU skates up to BETTY.

LOU: Bethany!

BETTY: Oh, Lou, it's like fairyland. Look at the snow glistening in the lights. It's beautiful! Are you really my shining prince?

LOU: Of course.

They kiss.

BETTY: I'm so happy. This is wonderful.

LOU: It's wonderful. Full of glittery things to buy.

BETTY: I feel like a child in a toy shop.

LOU: Which toy shall I buy you first? You can have whatever you like!

BETTY: We can have whatever we want.

LOU: Whenever we want it.

BETTY: Exactly when we want it. We live in paradise. Bethany Paradise lives in paradise.

LOU: And we have money to buy toys. You make money so I have money and we have a nice apartment.

BETTY: With nice furniture.

LOU: And we have a car. And it'll go on and on.

BETTY: And on and on.

LOU: The show should run and run. And all the while we'll have nice things. (*He picks up one of the mannequins and starts dancing with her and talking to her.*)

LOU: What do you say honey? Where tonight, The Ritz? (*He sings 'Putting on the Ritz'.*)

BETTY: Lou! How long do you think the show will run?

LOU: Years.

BETTY: How many years?

LOU: Five at least. (*He takes the mannequin back to her place and picks up another.*)

BETTY: Five years in the same show!

LOU: Where shall we do our Christmas shopping, dear? Macy's or Bloomingdales?

BETTY: How many nights is that?

LOU (*putting the mannequin back*): Thousands.

BETTY: Thousands.

LOU: Being a star, playing the lead.

They skate on the spot, facing the audience.

BETTY: Being a star on Broadway.

LOU: Making money, being famous, living the high life – that's what it's about.

BETTY: Is it?

LOU: It's what you want. It's what you come here for. What you were born to do, Bethany Paradise.

BETTY stands still, in shock, as LOU smiles and continues skating on the spot.

Scene Three

Bethany Paradise's star dressing room, towards the end of a matinée. BETTY is reading a letter from Amelia, SHIRLEY is hovering in the background, preparing a costume for the finale. AMELIA is upstage – an ethereal figure.

AMELIA: Dear Betty, I came to see your show and I enjoyed your performance.

BETTY: Shirley! Shirley! She came to see me! She was there!

AMELIA: It was such a happy, uplifting show – we truly need some jolliness in these dark times of the depression. You've gotten quite famous...

BETTY (*reading*): 'It was lovely to see your name outside the theatre shining in the night – although it took me a while to realise that Bethany Paradise was you. It took me a while to realise who you were on stage too, born and bred in Brooklyn, I thought....' Oh, Shirley! She believed in me, she thought I was American! (*She continues to read:*) 'No sign of that little girl dancing on the beach in Burry Port, it was all so glamorous and glitzy.' You were there, Amelia! You came to see me. Shirley! Shirley! Amelia Earhart came, she came to see the show.

SHIRLEY: Amelia Earhart saw the show? No kidding! Now get your costume on, it's finale time.

AMELIA: Now I'm gonna let you in on something. I've decided to fly around the world. Its all pretty confidential at the moment so let it be our secret. This will be the greatest adventure of my life.

154

BETTY (*in a reverie of long ago*): I knew she would. I've waited for ever for this. She said she would, in a letter long ago... it was just before my very first performance.

SHIRLEY: If you don't get this costume on, this'll be your last.

SHIRLEY helps BETTY into her costume.

BETTY: The first time I ever danced on stage – in front of an audience – I was wearing a blue chiffon dress.

SHIRLEY: I've always loved blue chiffon. Now come on honey, we don't have much time.

BETTY (*remembering Amelia's letter of long ago*): 'I'll be one in a hundred, or maybe thousands, you won't know where I am..'

SHIRLEY: I know where you should be.

BETTY: I'm trying to remember the rest of the letter.

SHIRLEY: Try to remember the rest of the show.

SHIRLEY continues to fix and fasten, as BETTY stands in a dream.

BETTY: 'You won't know where I am, you'll just know I'm there watching you and...

As BETTY falters, AMELIA – who all along has been an ethereal figure upstage – takes over.

AMELIA: Marvelling, spellbound by the precision of your movements.

BETTY joins in.

AMELIA and BETTY: Your beauty, your fragile elegance and the poetry of the emotions you express.

SHIRLEY: I knew I shouldn't 'ave given you that letter. (*She fastens a cummerbund and adds the final touches to a glitzy, feathery costume.*)

Off-stage, we hear the finale music. AMELIA disappears.

SHIRLEY: Come on, your public's waiting.

BETTY stands in a trance.

SHIRLEY: Can't you hear the music?

BETTY: Janey'll have to go on.

SHIRLEY: What?!

BETTY: She's my understudy.

SHIRLEY: Are you crazy? It's the walk-down, the finale, the curtain call, for god sakes!

BETTY: I don't want to do it.

SHIRLEY: Come on it's your favourite part, you always said. All that applause.

BETTY: That's the problem Shirley, it is, it is my favourite part. It's the only part I've been enjoying for months now. (*She mimes the end of her finale dance, the walk down, the curtain call.*) Oh, they like me, Oh, I've pleased them. They love me!

SHIRLEY: Of course they do! You're a roaring success.

BETTY (*blows kisses to the audience, then stops*): It's not beautiful, Shirley, it's not fragile or elegant and it's certainly not poetic. That's what Amelia saw. And its not a grand adventure. (*She begins dismantling her costume.*)

SHIRLEY (*grabbing the letter*): Hold on! Wait a minute! It says here, 'Happy, uplifting show, jolliness... wonderful performance.'

BETTY: Performance – yes, that's exactly it. I certainly perform – like an animal in the circus, I repeat pretty patterns over and over and boy do I do it well! I may as well be in the circus, Shirley!

SHIRLEY (*still reading*): 'You've gotten quite famous.'

BETTY: Yes, but what for?

SHIRLEY: 'It was lovely to see your name in lights.'

BETTY: But it's not my name, don't you see?! Now call Janey, Shirley, we can't let the audience down, they've paid good money to see the sparkly costumes and the painted smiles.

BETTY is putting on her civvies. SHIRLEY grabs the costume and, on the way out, bumps into LOU.

LOU: What in God's name?!

SHIRLEY: Leave her alone, Lou Daniels.

LOU: Are you sick or crazy?

SHIRLEY: There's nothing wrong with her. (*She exits.*)

LOU: She's lost her mind. There's a theatre full of people out there. What do you think you're doing?

BETTY: Janey'll be fine.

LOU: You are completely crazy. What are you doing?

BETTY: Packing my things.

LOU: Are you walking out?

BETTY: What does it look like?

LOU: No one, no one walks out on a show.

BETTY: I just did.

LOU: Get back on that stage.

BETTY: The show's over, Lou.

LOU: Aw! Come on honey, have a drink.

LOU pours two whiskies. BETTY gets her coat. LOU offers BETTY a drink but she walks past him.

BETTY: No thanks.

LOU (*he drinks her drink, himself.*): How are you going to live?

BETTY: I'll find a way.

LOU: All those meetings. The connections we made. We were on our way to the stars.

BETTY: I want to dance, Lou.

LOU: Hollywood was calling.

BETTY: I'm a dancer.

LOU: They have dancers in Hollywood.

BETTY: I can't do it, Lou.

LOU: Aw, I get it now! You're frightened. Don't be afraid, lil' darlin'. Lou Daniels is with you, I'll guide you every inch of the way. I love you, Bethany.

BETTY: I love you too, Lou.

LOU: You are the most beautiful, the most amazing woman in this whole goddam world.

BETTY Do you think so?

LOU: Don't be afraid of fame.

BETTY: I have become someone else.

LOU: You're so talented.

BETTY: It was so easy.

LOU: It comes naturally to you.

BETTY: Night after night after night.

LOU: They can't get enough of you.

BETTY: I feel like a bauble that catches the light.

LOU: What?

BETTY: I've woven myself a colourful cloak.

LOU: Stop this.

BETTY: And I have made myself invisible.

LOU: You're a star.

BETTY: There's something inside me.

LOU: Oh no, no, tell me you're not.

BETTY: Dreams! Desires, Lou.

LOU: You read too many books. Go home and get a good night's sleep and you'll feel better in the morning.

BETTY: No, you don't understand. I'm a fool and I'm a liar.

LOU: That's showbiz, honey. We fool them, we lie to them and they give us their gold. Pretty damn good, eh?

BETTY: No, no, no.

Pause.

LOU: What is it? Can't you take the pressure? Go on then, give it all up and go back where you came from, to that dull little village on the edge of the world.

160

BETTY: I'm not giving up, and I'm not going home. This is my home now. I'm just leaving the show.

LOU: If you leave the show you leave me.

BETTY: What?

LOU: You say no to the show you say no to me.

BETTY: They're two separate things.

LOU: I'm your agent, Beth.

BETTY: You said you loved me.

LOU: That's the deal.

BETTY: Loving someone isn't a business contract.

LOU: I love you 'cos you're you and you are Bethany Paradise.

BETTY: I'm not, that's my stage name, that's not me – I'm Betty Parry.

LOU: Not any more you're not.

BETTY: You don't own me, Lou.

LOU: You left her behind you a long time ago.

BETTY: This isn't making sense.

LOU: It makes perfect sense to me. Everyone has bills to pay.

BETTY: You'll have to find someone else to lay your golden eggs. This golden goose is leaving.

LOU: You can't mean it. You're throwing everything away. You'll be nothing. You'll be nobody and you'll wake up one morning and realise what a terrible mistake you've made.

BETTY: I want a grand adventure. A shining adventure.

LOU: Don't be ridiculous.

BETTY: Goodbye, Lou.

Scene Four

Carnegie Hall.

AMELIA (*giving a speech*): We must dream if the human race is to have a future and our dreams should know no bounds. Ladies and Gentlemen, I am a firm believer in international co-operation to secure the end to war; the cause of international peace and freedom transcends all boundaries. Similarly, there should be no boundaries for men and women. Women's rights must be made theirs, that is by constitutional guarantee.

BETTY enters.

AMELIA: We must aim for utopia. President Roosevelt's social polices are transforming America, and he has done more for women than any previous president. Recently I was privileged to be a guest at the White House and I saw Martha Graham transcend the boundaries of dance. She told us about Isadora Duncan and the 'vibration of the

American soul soaring upwards' and Ruth St Denis and the 'inner reality of the spiritual being,' the 'exquisite moments of the hidden self.'

AMELIA (*addressing BETTY, directly*): And the 'spontaneous dance of every child,' and I thought of you on the beach in Wales. This is a time of change, Betty. New winds are blowing, new art, poetry and music, new dance, new mountains to climb. Maybe you'll follow in the footsteps of the great innovators of dance – Isadora Duncan, Ruth St Denis, Martha Graham... maybe you're ready for the next peak.

The light fades, slowly.

Scene Five

Shirley's tenement apartment.

BETTY (*clutching a book and knocking loudly on the door to Shirley's apartment*): Shirley, Shirley.

SHIRLEY (*emerges wearing a dressing gown and a scarf on her head*): Alright, alright, I'm coming. No need to break the door down. (*She opens the door.*) Beth.

BETTY: Shirley...

SHIRLEY: Don't come to me asking for a job. I'm not Mr Ziegfeld.

BETTY: I just wanted to ask you some questions.

SHIRLEY: Nothing personal I hope.

BETTY: Have you heard of Isadora Duncan?

SHIRLEY: Have I heard of Isadora Duncan? She's my mother.

BETTY half-believes her.

SHIRLEY: Only kidding. Come in, but keep your voice down. There are people sleeping in this apartment.

BETTY (*whispering*): I found this book in a dime-store. It's called 'My Life' by Isadora Duncan. She had a vision of America dancing a dance.

SHIRLEY: I'll go and make us some cocoa.

BETTY: No thank you. Here it is. (She reads:) 'I see America dancing standing with one foot on the Rockies, her two hands stretched from Atlantic to Pacific, her fine head tossed to the sky, her forehead shining with a crown of a million stars....' That's me, Shirley. That's how I'm going to dance. I have to meet this Isadora. You must tell me where she is.

SHIRLEY: Too late, honey. She died a while back.

BETTY: Oh no. Do you know anything about her?

SHIRLEY: Yes.

BETTY: Well, tell me all about her then.

SHIRLEY: Once upon a time...

BETTY: I don't want fairy stories.

SHIRLEY: This ain't no fairy story. This is changing the world.

BETTY: I knew it!

SHIRLEY: She died when the fringe of her scarf got caught in the spokes of her Bugati. It was in the south of France, in 1927. She was a pretty wild kid.

BETTY: Did you ever see her dance?

SHIRLEY: Yes. All her movements were inspired by the waves 'cos she was born by the sea.

BETTY: That's me! I was born by the sea.

SHIRLEY: She was a complete screwball, Betty. She wore sandals and a Grecian tunic. She had too many lovers. They adored her in Russia.

BETTY: I knew you'd know! And have you heard of Ruth St Denis?

SHIRLEY is silent.

BETTY: Have you, Shirley? Have you heard of Ruth St Denis and her school with Ted Shaun? What was it called now?

SHIRLEY: Aw, Denishawn.

BETTY: Yes. So you have heard of her?

SHIRLEY: They were all screwballs. Leave it alone, its too dangerous.

BETTY: How can dancing be dangerous?

SHIRLEY: Leave it where it is. It'll go away in time.

BETTY: I want to dance on the Rockies, I want to wear a crown of a million stars, I want to feel the vibration of the American soul soaring upwards.

SHIRLEY: How about that cocoa?

BETTY: I want to make a dance that's free!

SHIRLEY: Forget free, there's no such thing.

BETTY: Of course there is.

SHIRLEY: Keep your life predictable then you'll be free. Don't go chasing rainbows, it'll only end in tears.

BETTY: I don't think like that. If I thought like that I'd end up... I don't want to end up...

SHIRLEY: As a dresser on a Broadway show.

BETTY: Oh no, I didn't mean that.

SHIRLEY: Of course you did.

BETTY: No, no!

SHIRLEY: What's wrong with being a dresser?

BETTY: Nothing.

SHIRLEY: It's not that bad being a dresser on a Broadway show. What's wrong with Broadway shows? (*She dances, Broadway-style. It is mostly parody; sad and tawdry.*) What's wrong with loud and colourful, glamour and glitz? What's wrong with teeth and smiles?

BETTY: I'm sorry Shirley. I thought I could talk to you. I thought you 'd understand. I'd better go.

SHIRLEY: No, don't go.

BETTY: I always thought there was this 'something else' with you. I don't know why. I always thought you didn't really...

SHIRLEY: Buy into the crap. You're right. I don't. I see right through it. I saw right through it a long time ago kid. You want some cocoa now?

BETTY: Talk to me Shirley!

SHIRLEY: OK, ok. If you must know I studied at Denishawn with Miss Ruth.

BETTY: You studied with Ruth St Denis?

SHIRLEY: I was like you then, full of hope... but there were other things, you know... people... there was this guy... my family... they wanted stuff from me... you know...

BETTY: How did that stop you dancing?

SHIRLEY: Gee, I don't know how they did it, but they made me feel as if I was indulging in some strange perversion. They said that dancers were all screwballs.

167

BETTY: Have you heard of Martha Graham?

SHIRLEY (*laughs*): Oh yeah! She's a screwball too.

Scene Six

Martha Graham's Studio.

MARTHA: My dancing is like a painting by Kandinsky – colourful, shocking, vibrant. I want you to walk across the floor with one arm above your head saying your name.

BETTY does so, saying 'Betty Parry'.

MARTHA: Now I know everything about you. There are no mirrors, we must see with our souls, we do not count, we move on the rhythm of our breath.

BETTY dances as MARTHA teaches.

MARTHA: All life hangs on breath. Breathe in and breathe out. Your diaphragm sparks the gesture, propels the arms and legs, contract and release, ebb and flow, and keep your back straight, this is where the wings grow, and a spiral fall and wrap your flesh around your bones and turn your face away and you are invisible, move it back and the connection is as magic as any on this earth. With the dedication of a prayer with absolute truthfulness.

All that is important is this one moment, your whole life   is in this one moment, it comes from deep inside you, emotional, intense. It is morning in the Appallachians, it is spring, ecstasy fills your soul, we are dancing to the top of the mountain, it is Parnassus, we are drinking nectar, we are gods.

The dance stops.

MARTHA: The American Indians. Our roots. Deep, deep inside. Our very souls are infused with the spiritual experiences of the first peoples to roam these lands. They are me. They are you. They are all of us. Bring me a dance about the Navajo.

BETTY dances.

MARTHA: The butterfly woman of the Navajo in the house of light and rainbows, washing in the magic water of the giant white sea shell, making feathers dance, swallowing swords and playing with fire and not getting burned.

Yes, yes, that would be good, almost at the beginning – I like the strength and that's so lyrical, that slow rhythmic slide, the relationship of the primitive with the earth.

BETTY stops dancing.

MARTHA: No, no, don't stop, show me that again.

BETTY does so, then continues with fast prancing and stepping.

MARTHA: Yes that is exciting! That rapid tempo change for the victory movement.

BETTY: No, that's the fire, it's when she finds...

MARTHA: It would be good at the climax.

BETTY: But it's all one dance.

MARTHA: There are some beautiful movements. Yes some of them are very interesting.

BETTY: One leads to the next. You always say remember where you've come from, each movement leads inevitably to the next, it's a chain, they're all linked...

MARTHA: Wait a minute.

BETTY: You wanted me to make a dance.

MARTHA: Yes and you have and it is beautiful and I want to use some of the movements and you should be flattered.

BETTY: It begins, it develops, it has it's own climax. I was born by the sea, and when I was a little girl...

MARTHA: I don't need to know that, Betty.

BETTY: I've always felt that water, washing, was magical.

MARTHA: That is not what is interesting! What is interesting is that you have one note, Betty. I have worked hard to develop that particular note. I need many, many notes to create my symphony.

BETTY (*dancing again*): You say this is all one note.

MARTHA: You know damn well what I mean, I won't waste my time here, I have important work to do. I take what I want, you do as I say, this is my vision. The whole meaning of your life depends on the authenticity of my work. I use you totally or not at all.

BETTY: Not at all.

The lights snap off.

Scene Seven

BETTY is walking through the streets of New York, at night. AMELIA appears, sitting in the desert.

BETTY: Dear Amelia, I'm working in a hat shop on Fifth Avenue. I thought of you shopping for hats in Boston in your blue Roadster. Sometimes I stand outside the theatre where I had my name in lights and I see Lou and Shirley walking past.

The light cross fades to reveal:

Scene Eight

The Californian desert, on a starlit night.

AMELIA: Dear Betty, I thought of you as I booked my mother a passage on the Red Star Lines Western Land. She's sailing to Europe this summer. I wanted you to know that my crack-up at Honolulu was nothing. It seemed I hit a wet spot and the ship began to go off-course. The load was too heavy. I cut the switches. Crack-ups – they happen.

BETTY: I don't want to go back, but I don't know how to go forward.

AMELIA: I'm sitting looking at the stars in the middle of the Californian desert. A tiny speck in a vast emptiness.

BETTY: I'm stuck. Stuck in the middle of nowhere.

AMELIA: People ask me, am I going on? I've got a reputation to defend, and what about commitment, honesty and courage? All those people that have worked so hard to help me?

BETTY: I danced so people would like me. I founded my life on the desire to be told I'm good.

AMELIA: It's not about that public success. If I had my way I'd be out of the public eye – I'm not exploiting the nation for fame and fortune.

BETTY: People paid me for pleasing them.

AMELIA: I make no money from it. I raise the money to pay for the flight and everything that goes with it – ten autographs before orange juice, fifteen before bacon and eggs, twenty-five more before retiring – the publicity raises money, that's why I do it. It's hard work.

BETTY: But to be really good I must please myself.

AMELIA: I'm gonna please myself. I'm flying round the world because I want to and it looks like the only way I'll get some peace.

BETTY: I feel I have no self to please. Can you see me Amelia? I can't see myself?

AMELIA (*referring to her own feelings, too*): I strain to see your little flame inside, the flame that burnt so brightly on the beach in Burry Port.

BETTY: I want to create a form of dance that is totally unique to me and me alone.

AMELIA: Then do it.

BETTY: What if it's no good?

AMELIA: It will be.

BETTY: Someone needs to tell me where to start.

AMELIA: Tell yourself.

BETTY: I can't.

AMELIA: Why not? If you want to make your own dances.

BETTY: Wanting's not enough.

AMELIA: You've done so much, you've got this far.

BETTY: That wasn't me. It was someone else pretending to be me. I'm afraid.

AMELIA: What are you afraid of? Stand right there and say it out loud. What are you afraid of? Some people are afraid of rooms full of strangers. Some people are afraid of wasps and bees – sure they sting, or spiders that don't, or umbrellas – they can give you a nasty poke in the eye. What are you afraid of?

Pause.

BETTY: I'm afraid of being me.

AMELIA: Now look here young lady, you're you and that's an end to it, so just be you. Who are you anyway?

No answer.

AMELIA: What's your name?

BETTY: Betty Parry.

AMELIA: And where are you from?

BETTY: Burry Port, Carmarthenshire, Wales.

AMELIA: There you are then. It's all you've got. And we ain't got long, so don't waste time.

BETTY: Who wants to know about my life?

AMELIA: Do it and find out. Don't let the past entrap you, don't put your faith in a tomorrow that never comes. Reading about other people's dreams in books is no substitute for your own. Act on your dreams, Betty – your dreams, it's your story, no one else's.

BETTY: If I open the door I'll be washed away. All my desires running deep like an underground stream. I'm afraid that they'll burst and I'll be swept aside and drowned. I'm so afraid. I'm not brave like you. I can't touch your angel's wings.

AMELIA: Do you think I don't feel fear? Now under the stars, waiting for take off.

BETTY: The long white road across the heavens, the path the spirits take as they leave the earth.

AMELIA: I must believe the stars will guide me. Oh yes I feel fear, as I clutch my thermos flask and my box of sandwiches. I put on a jolly smile when I wave goodbye, but my fear consumes me. But then I get in the plane and

174

start the engine and when the plane starts to taxi down the runway my fear goes, I leave it behind me and then I fly, I leave the...

BETTY joins in.

AMELIA and BETTY: Sorrows of the world behind me, even the small sorrow of the rain.

BETTY gets up and dances. It is a slow dance of longing which develops into a triumphant dance of freedom.

AMELIA: Don't be afraid of your deepest desires, feelings can't hurt you, and there's no right or wrong, no one can tell you what to do, you have to find that out for yourself. It's not about escaping anymore. It's not about control and it's not for sheer pleasure, it's the only way to be free. It's for freedom from now on.

Scene Nine

Miami Airport, 1937.

AMELIA – about to embark on her round the world flight – is addressing a crowd of journalists. BETTY is among them.

AMELIA: Some people think I'm mad to attempt this flight, but it's a very personal desire. I want to, I need to, make this final gesture before I give up long-distance stunt flying for good. If I'm forced down I sure hope I don't land in the African Jungle – too many lions and tigers for me, not to mention snakes. Now the Pacific Ocean's different, there are desert islands there. I find that quite appealing – shady palm trees, and white beaches.

You'll all be glad to know I'll be writing a daily account of my adventures exclusively for the New York Herald Tribune. I have a gut feeling there's this one last trip left in me and when I finish this job I mean to settle down for keeps. I mean to enjoy my lovely home in the Californian sun, read lots of books and see my friends. I'm choosing the longest possible distance around the equator, traversing the world at its waist, so I won't be competing with existing records. Lastly, I have a confession to make, I have a small and probably feminine horror of growing old, so you can be sure I won't feel completely cheated if I fail to comeback. Wish me luck; and remember, women must now and then do things to show what women can do.

BETTY: Good luck, Amelia. Good luck, Amelia Earhart.

AMELIA waves, her scarf flying in the wind.

BETTY: God speed. Safe journey.

BETTY watches, as AMELIA disappears. The light fades, isolating BETTY in a pool of light.

BETTY: I came to tell you that I'm going home. I see myself on a sandy shore, long stretches of surf caressing the beach, licking it, kissing it, longing for it, embracing it and letting it go with a long singing sigh. I am walking on the dunes waving at the trains, where the sea thrift and the thistles grow. I am standing in the sea with the urchins and the eels, jellyfish and cockles, my toes squeeze the wet sand, seaweed bracelets bind my ankles, I am filling my lungs with saltiness and, oh, how I long for home.

Scene Ten

The beach and pub, Burry Port, June 14th, 1937.

BETTY has just arrived home. Sheets are hanging on the line. She stands on the beach, grown-up and shiny, suitcase in hand. Lights go up in the pub. She sees an older, more tired ROSE, ironing sheets. Eventually, ROSE realises someone is watching her. She looks up and sees BETTY. The two women smile and, slowly, walk towards each other.

ROSE: Well, who's this grown up stranger? Why didn't you tell me you were coming?

BETTY: You'd have baked a cake.

ROSE: I'd have gone down Miss Jones's for a Battenburg.

BETTY: Have you won the pools?

ROSE: Come here.

They embrace.

BETTY: I missed you, mam.

ROSE: Oh, and I missed you. Why have you come home? Is everything alright?

BETTY: Never been better.

ROSE: Is it a holiday?

BETTY No, it's work.

ROSE: There's no work here. Even Madame's retired.

BETTY: So there's no dancing school.

ROSE: No.

BETTY: Once upon a time in the Land of Sheets where everything was shiny white...

ROSE: There lived a beautiful princess called Sparkling Betty.

BRIAN (*off-stage*): Rose, Rose. (*He arrives.*) Betty!

BETTY: Hello Brian.

BRIAN: Well if it isn't the one and only – welcome home. It's the New York Herald Tribune. It's Amelia's first piece.

BETTY: Read it to me, Brian.

BRIAN: Forgotten how, have you?

ROSE: I'll read it.

BETTY: Mam! So you've been following Amelia's progress in the papers.

ROSE: Of course, and yours as well. We've got all the cuttings.

BETTY: Do you have to hide them under the bed?

Pause.

BETTY: It's alright, Mam. I can face Danny.

ROSE: You won't have to.

BETTY: I'm not afraid anymore.

Pause.

BETTY: What's wrong? He's gone, hasn't he? Has he gone?

ROSE: He drowned. He walked into the sea. He said his head was full of screams. I cried at first – the tears I couldn't cry before, for all the years of hoping I could change him. I work the same but now I get to keep the money. I'm sorry Betty, it wasn't right.

BETTY: It's alright Mam. We'll have flouncy chiffon frocks and peaches and cream.

They hug.

BRIAN: Come on now. Let me read Amelia's piece. (*He reads:*) 'I put the Electra into a slow climb...'

ROSE and BETTY join in and they all read.

ROSE, BETTY and BRIAN: 'Then headed for Puerto Rico where the deep blue of the gulf stream met the aquamarine of the shoal waters off coast.'

Scene Eleven

Madame's house/studio, July 2nd, 1937.

It is the day AMELIA gets lost. MADAME sits down. BETTY reads from the Herald Tribune.

MADAME: 'Then Caripito, Venezuela, where we ate steak and fruitcake and the orchids grow wild, then Paramaribo Dutch Guiana, and in San Juan I had a curious feeling I had been there before.'

BETTY: I'm going to create something truly revolutionary.

MADAME: 'The Red Sea which belied its name being blue and the blue and white Niles equally deceitful, being green.' Ah, she is so witty, Miss Earhart.

BETTY: I want my dance to change the world.

MADAME: 'In the distance I sighted a shimmering land of mirages that was Arabia....' 'My first sight of Rangoon...'

BETTY: I'm not American. I'm Welsh. American history meant something deep to Martha, these visceral emotions about frontiers people and American Indians, they weren't in me.

MADAME: Pah, this Graham way.

BETTY: And her technique didn't work on my body easily because of my bone structure. We're all so different, everything we are has evolved from our life history, race memory, every individual has her own code in space and time, that is the material of choreography and it's the Parry Way in Wales.

MADAME: Why don't you change your name? Paritski's nice.

BETTY: I'm not Russian, either. I compose on my own body and everything this body is, owns, wants, needs, remembers. I'll draw my movements out of the earth, the ever-changing life around me.

MADAME: The earth of Burry Port! The ever-changing life! Dance was born in the palaces of kings and queens. Its soul is beauty. Its essence truth. Its heart heroic.

BETTY: That is all around me.

MADAME: Where?

BETTY: In the spiritual experiences of the first peoples to roam these lands. In the doomed lovers Nest and Rhys on the bridge of screams. In brave Gwenllian defending her castle. In the waves of the sea, in my mother's life.

BRIAN (*entering, at speed*): Madame! Betty! Turn the radio on, Amelia's on the radio!

BETTY moves to turn on the radio. Amelia's bandana falls to the floor.

MADAME: And you still carry that old thing around with you.

We hear music – the end of a programme. BETTY picks up the bandana and sits opposite MADAME.

NEWSCASTER'S VOICE: At 10:22 this morning Amelia Earhart and her navigator Fred Noonan made a successful

181

take off from Lae Aerodrome Papua New Guinea. They were bound for Howland island on the last leg of their round the world flight. Miss Earhart, the Queen of the Air, has already flown two thousand, five hundred and sixty miles in thirty days in her silver plane, the Lockheed Electra, using a thousand gallons of petrol.

Towards the end of the news bulletin there is crackling and distortion. The stage darkens. We hear clearly AMELIA's voice on the Lockheed radio.

AMELIA (*on radio*): A. Earhart. Overcast. Will listen on 3105 kilocycles on hour and half-hour.

Interference.

AMELIA (*on radio*): Partly cloudy.

Static.

AMELIA (*on radio*): Want bearing on 3105 kilocycles on hour will whistle in microphone. (*She whistles but it is indistinguishable from the whining sounds of Pacific radio reception at dawn.*)

Scene Twelve

AMELIA is sitting in the cockpit of her plane, in cloud, silhouetted against the sheets and BETTY, tossing and turning in bed.

AMELIA (*on stage and on plane radio*): Please take bearing on us and report in half an hour. I'll make noise in microphone. About one hundred miles out...

182

Interference.

AMELIA: We must be on you but cannot see you but gas is running low. Been unable to reach you by radio. We are flying at altitude 1000 feet. Only one half hour gas left.

BETTY: It's dark... there's mist...

Interference.

AMELIA (*her voice becoming shrill and breathless, the words tumbling over one another*): Earhart calling Itasca. We are circling but cannot hear you. Go ahead on 7500 either now or on schedule time on half hour. KHAQQ calling Irasca. We received your signals but unable to get a minimum bearing. Please take bearing on us and answer on 3105 with voice.

BETTY: It's cold... freezing, must be the wind.

AMELIA: We are in the line of position 156 dash 137 6210 kilocycles. We are running north and south.

The hum of the plane stops. All sounds stop. Immediately, AMELIA is heard shouting incoherently and intermittently into the microphone, as BETTY moans and gasps in her nightmare.

AMELIA (*incoherent, drowned by sound*): KHAQQ calling Itasca.

BETTY: No sun, no stars.

Silence.

AMELIA (*incoherent, drowned by sound*): Please take bearing.

Silence.

AMELIA (*incoherent, drowned by sound*): No gas left.

Weak morse code signals: LA... A... T... followed by indecipherable transmissions then SOS, SOS, SOS, KHAQQ, KHAQQ. Complete silence and darkness. A blood-curdling scream.

Scene Thirteen

Betty's bedroom.

BETTY is sitting up in bed, screaming. ROSE rushes in.

ROSE: Are you alright, Betty?

BETTY: I dreamt I died, mam. Am I dead? Have I gone to heaven? Are you here too?

ROSE: I'm here and you're here and we're not in heaven, we're at home.

BETTY: I was lost. I'd lost all sense of direction. There was a strong east wind, a cold wind. There was a mist all round me, it was dark. Then I realised that I was flying through the air. I was in the sky but there was no sun. It was night but there were no stars and I was being propelled forward faster than the speed of light. It took my breath away and then I was falling... falling... falling... aaaaaah... through the darkness, through the cloud, a long way and then I was no more. I disappeared, I died. Oh, mam, it was terrible. I'm still in it. I can't get out of this. (*She cries.*)

ROSE: Ssh. It's alright, it's alright, it was only a dream, a bad dream. Everybody has them now and again, they're not real, they don't mean anything.

BETTY: It was real. I'm dead mam, I'm dead.

ROSE: I'll get you a cup of hot milk.

BETTY: My heart's beating, I can see you...

ROSE: You'll be better in the morning.

BETTY: I'm cold.

ROSE: Come into my room.

BETTY: Bring more blankets.

ROSE: Betty, it was a bad dream. That's all.

BETTY: No stars, no sun.

ROSE: You've been working too hard.

BETTY: No breath.

ROSE: That new fangled dancing, it goes too deep.

BETTY (*screams suddenly, as though she were falling*): Help me, I'm falling, I'm falling.

ROSE: I'm holding you, I'm holding you.

BETTY flails and wails.

ROSE: Let me hold you. I'm here. I'm here.

ROSE holds BETTY until she relaxes and is quiet.

ROSE: Go to sleep now.

BETTY: No.

ROSE: It's alright, it's gone now. Go to sleep.

BETTY: I can't, I'm afraid.

ROSE: Try to forget.

BETTY: I can't.

ROSE: Close your eyes.

BETTY (*closes her eyes, then opens them immediately*): Black mist is swirling all around me, and there's thunder and there's lightning, ice on my wings, I'm flying low above the white-caps. I can't see any more. (*She is suddenly exhausted.*)

Scene Fourteen

Morning – the pub.

There is loud banging on the door. ROSE opens it. It is BRIAN.

BRIAN: Rose.

ROSE: What time is it?

BRIAN: Bad news.

ROSE: What's wrong?

BRIAN: Amelia Earhart's missing.

BETTY enters. She is drained, listless.

BRIAN: Sit down, Betty.

BETTY: What for?

ROSE: It's Amelia.

BETTY: What about her?

BRAIN: Howland's a speck in the ocean, Betty. Do you know what size it is?

BETTY: Two miles long and half a mile wide, twenty foot at it's highest.

BRIAN: It'd be like landing on a beach, Cefn Sidan Sands.

Pause.

BRIAN: She hasn't landed on Howland, Betty.

BETTY: Where is she then?

BRIAN: No one knows.

Pause.

BRIAN: They don't know if she's landed yet.

BETTY: Who's 'they'?

187

BRIAN: The United States government. They started searching straight away. The Navy's out. Probably the Herald Tribune desperate for the next installment.

Pause.

BRIAN: Eleanor Roosevelt said she hoped they'd find her because she thought of her as a wonderful person and a friend far more than a pilot or an adventurer.

MADAME (*enters*): Betty, I came to tell you... what's wrong?

BRIAN: Amelia Earhart's missing. She ran out of fuel.

MADAME: *Ma petite*!

ROSE: They're bound to find her.

MADAME: *Bien sur*.

BRIAN: The Electra's a seaplane. If she's come down on the sea, the plane's got enough buoyancy to float.

BETTY: She's not going to land on the sea.

ROSE: The Friendship did.

BRIAN: She's got a life raft.

BETTY: Amelia doesn't need a life raft.

BRIAN: If something's gone wrong... Betty, there was a message... Amelia's voice on the radio... she was running out of fuel. I've brought some maps.

BETTY (*smiling as she speaks, she has the bandana and the poem in her hand*): She's sitting on the banks of a blue lagoon drinking coconut milk, dangling her feet in the water. The sky is azure blue, not a cloud in sight and birds of paradise are singing in the palm trees. She is smiling her big white-toothed smile, her blue eyes dancing. The warmth seeps into every part of her body. She breathes the perfume of exotic flowers.

Scene Fifteen

The beach, sixteen days later.

BRIAN has a large map of the South Seas – which he is attempting to show BETTY – and piles of newspapers. MADAME and ROSE sit, watching.

BRIAN: Thousands and thousands of islands. The Marshalls here, here the Gilbert and Ellice islands. So see here this is Howland.

BETTY: I know Brian.

BRIAN: This is Lae in Papua New Guinea. This is where she flew from. And this is what she wrote before she flew...

BETTY and BRIAN: 'Not much more than a month ago, I was on the other side of the Pacific, looking westward. This evening, I look eastward over the Pacific.'

BRIAN: She flew over the Solomon Islands and Nukumanu. Over the Gilberts.

BETTY: They'll never find her.

BRIAN: Four thousand men manning ten ships and sixty-five aeroplanes are combing two hundred and fifty thousand square miles of the Pacific.

BETTY: Not if they search for a million years. If I could have been there, I'd have found her. I wish I could have been there. I'd dive into the sea. I'd plumb the darkest depths of that vast ocean. I'd swim through gardens of coral and anemones. Through shoals of shining fish past shipwrecks and treasure chests I'd carry her body out to the air.

I should have flown there on the back of a moonbeam.

All these years I've seen her smiling on her golden eagle, flying out of the sun, battling with the elements, ice and snow. That she rose above her fear, that was the most important part – her brave heart – that's the image I had when I struggled – this brave heart – this alone woman – I thought if Amelia could do that I could do this, so much smaller, less difficult – she risked her life every time she flew, I couldn't touch her angels wings – but every time I danced, when I practised, every performance she led me smiling above the clouds.

When I went to look for Madame and I couldn't find her. When all the streets looked the same. When I walked in my faded dress and Madame found me shoes; and when Danny said he owned me. The Friendship took me to America, her golden wings got me to Broadway, that's all I saw in Martha's studio. I saw Amelia flying in the Friendship, flying blind over unbroken ocean, two thousand miles of unbroken ocean.

I believed in her.

ROSE: And she believed in you.

MADAME: Betty Parry, one-time ballerina, and star of Broadway. Now innovative creative dancer, revolutionary dancer, you are somebody who is a very good dancer.

ROSE: And Amelia was somebody who was a very good aviator. Not a saint, not a goddess. An ordinary woman who did extraordinary things.

BETTY: Like you mam, and you Madame.

BRIAN reads from the New York Times. BETTY becomes isolated in a spotlight.

BRIAN (*reading*): 'She wanted to dare all that a man would dare, and she took her life in the effort to get the final ecstasy out of it... one remembers the outward symbols of what she was. Perhaps in the vividness of her lost glimpse of sun and sky and the curling tops of waves, she knew that she had helped to make women less afraid.'

BETTY: I'm going to create a new form of dance. I'll teach, I'll have a studio, my own company, and I'm going to name it the 'Amelia Ear...'

AMELIA (*appearing as a ghostly figure*): Your dreams Betty, remember. This is your story, no one else's.

Pause.

BETTY: The 'Betty Parry Dance Company'. She is still with me. Amelia is still with me. Love travels back and forth across continents, across oceans of humpbacked whales, through jungles, my heart flies faster than a plane called Friendship, flies with the west wind, my heart curls its toes in the warm, golden sand. I lean my head back

191

to face the sun. I close my eyes, I hold her hand. We turn to each other and smile. And Amelia smiles because she knows I'll dance for her and many people after me will dance the way they do because Amelia Earhart landed here in 1928. I see Wales dancing, her fine head tossed to the sky, her forehead shining with a crown of a million stars. (*She dances.*)

AMELIA (*reciting her poem*):

> Courage is the price that life exacts for granting
> peace,
> the soul that knows it not knows no release from little
> things,
> knows not the livid loneliness of fear, nor mountain
> heights,
> where bitter joy can hear the sound of wings.
>
> How can Life grant us boon of living,
> compensate for dull grey ugliness and pregnant hate,
> Unless we dare
> The soul's dominion?
> Each time we make a choice we pay
> with courage to behold the restless day
> and count it fair.

The End.

Sian McDowall and Kath Dimery

photograph by Dave Daggers

HIJINX THEATRE

SPINNING THE ROUND TABLE
by Lewis Davies

A story of love and betrayal
set in the corridors of power

FOR COMMUNITY AUDIENCES [12]
On tour 20 September – 10 December 2005

CARDIFF
CAERDYDD

CYNGOR CELFYDDYDAU CYMRU
THE ARTS COUNCIL OF WALES
SUPPORTING CREATIVITY

Spinning the Round Table

Lewis Davies
in collaboration with
Chris Morgan

Spinning the Round Table was first performed at the Drama Studio, Whitchurch High School, Cardiff, on Tuesday 20th September 2005.

Cast:

Arthur/Reporter 3	–	Cerys Jones
Gwen/Kelly/Reporter 2	–	Alison John
Lawrence//Reporter 4	–	Morgan Rhys
Morgan/Victor Doyle /Reporter 1	–	Emyr John

Creative Team:

Director	–	Chris Morgan
Designer	–	Blaanid Maddrell
Music	–	James Williams
Lighting Designer Production Manager	–	Simon Gough
Stage Manager	–	Zsara Marshall

ACT ONE

A large pillar or plinth dominates a minimal stage set representing the central atrium of power. The pillar represents power and threat. It is capable of receiving both live and recorded images and projecting these to the audience. There is a 'designer' black settee and a podium. The rest of the set is grey and black; shadows and light.

The players are always watching each other. They rarely leave the stage but remain in the shadows.

ARTHUR enters. He walks to the podium and looks around. He checks and adjusts his suit, clears his throat. He is preparing to give a speech. He looks to the cameras/audience. Lights on him are adjusted, up and down.

ARTHUR: Thank you. It is my honour to be here tonight, to address the people of the country that have put their faith in me...

MORGAN enters. He motions for ARTHUR to continue.

ARTHUR: I am here to give my commitment to a vision of the future. A future of prosperity, a future of opportunity.... (*He stops. Looks to MORGAN.*) Have I got that right? Do you think we're overdoing the future?

MORGAN: It's good. The crowd will give you that extra lift. The cameras will love it.

ARTHUR: Are the networks carrying it live?

MORGAN: Just the state channel. The others are streaming it into the news reports.

ARTHUR: You are sure we've got the right feel to this speech?

MORGAN: Arthur, you have won a famous victory, we are celebrating.

ARTHUR: Some of the tone might seem... too sure.

MORGAN: The people will want some of our elation. They will want to feel part of the project, the time we have been promising them is here.

ARTHUR: We are to be a party of all the people.

MORGAN: Of course. Your sincerity will cut through all this... artifice. They believe in you.

ARTHUR: All those promises, Morgan, and now I have the chance to do something about them. I will keep the promises.

MORGAN: Of course....

ARTHUR: What time are we live?

MORGAN: Eight... the guests have begun to arrive.

ARTHUR: Have you seen Gwen?

MORGAN: She was doing an interview in the dressing room. *The Times*... they wanted a profile piece.

ARTHUR: She hasn't stopped working then?

MORGAN: It will give us an excellent front page, tomorrow.

ARTHUR: Good.

MORGAN: We need to put the information in front of the people.

ARTHUR: Of course. I will see if she has finished. (*He leaves.*)

MORGAN turns on the camera. The projector flashes into life, for the first time. It displays 'The Message', in white letters. MORGAN clicks it forward to a still of Arthur. He turns on the live feed, which shows the podium. He stands in front of it, his image projected on screen. He walks back to the camera and turns it off.

A rush of sound and flashes herald the start of the show – a gala opening. The audience has arrived in a swathe of flashlights and running beams which scour the auditorium.

MORGAN gets into performance mode.

MORGAN: Thank you all for coming tonight. We really want you to share in this sense of achievement and hope for the future that we have all worked for. It is to be a night of celebration, a night to reflect on our progress and to plan for the future. This is the beginning... the beginning of something good. I'm sure you'll all be keen to give our new President your full support. We're live at eight so please, the full nine yards. (*He leaves.*)

Background music – a loud rock anthem. ARTHUR and GWEN enter, through the audience. Lights and music heighten their entrance. They wave and shake hands with audience/cast members. ARTHUR stands at the podium. Arthur's image is projected, live, on screen. GWEN stands at his side. The music fades. ARTHUR composes himself, waiting for silence.

ARTHUR: Thank you. It is my honour to be here tonight, to address the people that have put their faith in me, in our party. I am here to give my commitment to the future that you have shown faith in. A future of prosperity and opportunity for all. A future of faith and consideration. I know from my travels in the last few weeks that it will be a difficult road. I have listened to you. Your concerns, opinions, ideas. My wife who has been at my side for the whole campaign has been the first to insist on listening to the people, your petitions.

It is her fortitude and strength that has sustained me. I would like to express my heartfelt thanks to her now. She has provided strength in difficult times and I am sure as we work together and move forward over the next few months we will reflect on the many wonderful moments that we have shared and it will give us both further strength to work towards the future.

A future that is brighter, a future that we can all share. There has been discord and disagreement for too long in the country. It is time for a change. Our shared problems of today will now become the successes of tomorrow as we will all participate in the opportunity of the future.

ARTHUR indicates for GWEN to join him. She does so.

Projection: 'More Applause' flashes on screen as an instruction to the crowd. Then, 'The Opportunity of the Future'.

Lights flash around the arena. ARTHUR and GWEN kiss.

Projection: The image on screen fades but remains in picture.

A single light falls on ARTHUR and GWEN. There is small flurry of confetti which falls around them. We see them in a slow motion dance, as time passes.

Lights return, illuminating ARTHUR and GWEN at the presidential home. ARTHUR looks at the image of himself, then turns off the screen with a remote control.

ARTHUR: Well, did you think we played it well?

GWEN: Do you think you had enough futures in that speech?

ARTHUR: Its our new catchphrase. 'The Opportunity of the Future.' Morgan thinks it will capture the imagination of the press.

GWEN: That shouldn't be too difficult.

ARTHUR: It's got a certain reasoning to it.

GWEN: Of course. I'm only teasing you.

ARTHUR: Your my wife, you're allowed. Do you think I still look like a young politician?

GWEN: I'd say you've developed the necessary level of gravitas.

ARTHUR: And style?

GWEN: Needs some direction... (*she touches him*) but with a certain uncertain charm.

ARTHUR: Do you realise we've won?

GWEN: I'm not sure yet. That was a long interview with *The Times*.

ARTHUR: Do you think we can have a few days off now? Tell the country thanks for the vote but do you mind if we take that holiday I booked in Tunisia.

GWEN: I'm not sure if it would be such a good idea.

ARTHUR crosses to the window. They begin a flirtation.

ARTHUR: The car is still there.

GWEN: Then they're waiting for us.

ARTHUR: There's a man at the door who I assume is security.

GWEN: Does he look like security?

ARTHUR: He looks rather robust.

GWEN: Do you really think we need to be protected? The people love you.

ARTHUR: There are always a few malcontents.

GWEN: I'm sure we will be able to convince them otherwise.

ARTHUR: I think you overestimate my power over the media.

GWEN: I think the media just got us elected.

ARTHUR: I never thought you were so cynical?

GWEN: I have to keep in touch with reality.

ARTHUR: And is this real? The flat, the new car, the man at the door to protect me from my people?

GWEN: It's part of the journey.

ARTHUR: You know when we were planning all this?

GWEN: Which bit?

ARTHUR: Me becoming elected. Our first election.

GWEN: To the student council.

ARTHUR: Yes, that one.

GWEN: Did you have to remind me?

ARTHUR: Did you mind losing?

GWEN: I was a victim of sexual discrimination.

ARTHUR: I behaved as a perfect gentleman. Even when you were questioning my parentage.

GWEN: That was the problem.

ARTHUR: It seemed to work.

GWEN: I realised you were a good deal.

ARTHUR: And now the people love me.

GWEN: No, I love you. (*She kisses him.*) They have realised you're a good deal.

ARTHUR: What's it like to be in love with the new leader?

GWEN: Just like the old leader.

ARTHUR: You were in love with him as well? (*He kisses her.*)

GWEN: I had to keep my options open.

ARTHUR: Ever the politician.

GWEN: Did you really think we'd win?

ARTHUR: Of course.

GWEN: Even when you lost all those early rounds?

ARTHUR: You've got to have faith... and a beautiful wife.

GWEN: Easy on the charm, you haven't offered me a job yet.

ARTHUR: Don't you think I'll keep my word?

GWEN: Everyone's an idealist until they're elected.

ARTHUR: And then?

GWEN: They become politicians.

ARTHUR: And what do you think of my performance so far?

GWEN: You've had your moments.

ARTHUR: I could not have done any of this without you.

GWEN: We've done it together.

ARTHUR: Yes.

GWEN: And now. What is there for us to do?

ARTHUR: There is much. Our dreams?

They break from their flirtation.

GWEN: The press are already talking about your new administration. Is Morgan going to be First Minister?

ARTHUR: I don't think so. I need someone who is a bit more media friendly. Morgan can control it but put him in front of the camera and you have a salesman. The people don't like salesmen.

GWEN: Then why not D'Lac? He'll certainly offer eager support.

ARTHUR: I don't know why you dislike Lawrence so much?

GWEN: I don't dislike him but I can't see anyone behind the politician.

ARTHUR: That's the job description.

GWEN: You'd think there was no humour in the man.

ARTHUR: He has a way with people. In front of their eyes he joins them from the screen. Not many people have that.

GWEN: It does nothing for me.

ARTHUR: He could become a great asset to us. The people need to be convinced of change.

GWEN: They will love you anyway.

ARTHUR: No, it is not as simple as that. Now they do. I have won. I have ideas. We have beaten a... bunch of losers. The mood can and will change. Someone like Lawrence can be very useful. As the leader you are always isolated. Sometimes you need to be isolated. He can bridge that gap.

GWEN: The charm he holds. It is too easy. People will see through it.

ARTHUR: Bit of contrast never did anyone any harm. I will have Morgan and Lawrence. Darkness and light. And I will be the centre. I will discuss it with Morgan in the morning.

GWEN: Then you have made the decision.

ARTHUR: Yes.

GWEN: Arthur? Our new relationship. I want to know how you feel about it?

ARTHUR: Very positive, there's a great future out there and we need to grasp the opportunity.

GWEN: I'm being serious.

ARTHUR: And so am I.

GWEN: Please, Arthur.

ARTHUR: I'm thinking about it. It's a delicate decision.

GWEN: I am aware of that.

ARTHUR: So I need some time to think about it.

GWEN: I need a proper role.

ARTHUR: Of course, we promised.

GWEN: I want to feel part of the new project.

ARTHUR: I'm sure we'll be able to find a useful position.

GWEN: Don't hide me behind some fundraising charity.

ARTHUR: The people see you in a special way. You are not tainted in the way I am as a politician. Through you the people can connect to us, to the party. We need to be aware of these advantages.

GWEN: What does that mean?

ARTHUR: It would be very difficult for you to have a party position. I would be your boss. I don't think that's appropriate.

GWEN: So?

ARTHUR: I can foresee some difficulties in line-management.

GWEN: Really?

ARTHUR: I could of course make an alternative proposal. Something less formal perhaps?

GWEN: Then I will accept.

ARTHUR: I haven't made it yet?

GWEN: I have confidence that you will make the right decision.

ARTHUR: Thank you. (*He kisses her.*)

GWEN: Yes, I.... It's been a long day. Have you finished working?

ARTHUR: We have a photo call at eleven.

GWEN: Then we need some sleep.

ARTHUR: No, not yet. You go ahead. I've a few letters to write.

GWEN leaves. The lights fade down, then up. ARTHUR is in his shirt sleeves, at his desk. He is working on a draft of a letter. There are newspapers stacked on the desk. MORGAN enters. He waits for ARTHUR to speak.

ARTHUR (*pointing to the newspapers*): It was a well-received speech, Morgan.

MORGAN: Thank you, sir. And the First Lady looks rather elegant.

ARTHUR: After a long campaign the journey is only just beginning for us.

MORGAN: Yes, time to put the promises we made into action.

ARTHUR: But is the party ready for the challenge, Morgan?

MORGAN: Yes, I'm sure we are, sir. We can succeed where the others have failed.

ARTHUR: Of course, everyone is eager. A thousand and one Knights, a thousand and one ideas. All rushing off on some personal crusade. (*Indicating letters on the desk:*) The petitions are already arriving.

MORGAN: I haven't had an opportunity to check my mail this morning.

ARTHUR: It is not a question of choice, you understand, these decisions we have to make. It is a question of getting the balance right. You know how fickle the people can be.

MORGAN: The people have been looking for leadership.

ARTHUR: The people do not know what they want. They know what they don't like.

MORGAN: So the reforms that we have promised. When do we start?

ARTHUR: It is necessary to get our internal structure in place. We've got the people. Now we need to get them in the right positions. Morgan, I value your opinion.

MORGAN: Thank you, sir.

ARTHUR: What do you think of Lawrence D'Lac?

MORGAN: He is a man of certain qualities... the highest integrity.

ARTHUR: A little arrogant?

MORGAN: Not... necessarily.

ARTHUR: Anything I should know about him that I don't?

MORGAN: He's dependable. A bit eager, given to making long speeches to anyone who will listen. He has been known to gamble on the horses and spend late nights at the casino losing a fortune.

ARTHUR: Really?

MORGAN: No, not really. That was a joke.

ARTHUR: Ah good, for a minute I thought I had got the wrong man.

MORGAN: He's a blank canvas. We can mould him to the party image.

ARTHUR: Good, exactly the qualities we need. I will be appointing him as First Minister.

MORGAN: First Minister?

ARTHUR: Yes?

MORGAN: I see.

ARTHUR: You seem... surprised?

MORGAN: It is the most important role in Government after the President. He will have great influence over our programme. He has no ministerial experience.

ARTHUR: Precisely.

MORGAN: The programme is likely to be unpopular in some quarters. The people are not always keen on sacrifice.

ARTHUR: I'm glad you understand the people so completely, Morgan, and of course their problems. It is why I think it is crucial that you remain as Director of Communications. The people will need to be convinced of these programmes. They need to be sold the benefits.

MORGAN: I was hoping to be more involved in their direct application, sir. I was thinking a ministerial role would be more fitting, useful...

ARTHUR: I need your expertise with the press. I can't afford to make mistakes at this point.

MORGAN: I think appointing Lawrence as First Minister is a mistake, sir.

ARTHUR: Why?

MORGAN: He is an outsider.

ARTHUR: What does that mean?

MORGAN: He is from an immigrant family.

ARTHUR: He was born here.

MORGAN: I am simply saying that, in certain sections of the press, his background will be discussed.

ARTHUR: Are you telling me, in this land of equality that we are trying to promote, I am not able to appoint Lawrence D'Lac?

MORGAN: He would be better employed in a less prominent position.

ARTHUR: And where would that be, in your opinion? The islands?

MORGAN: Lawrence is a talented man. But he is likely to become a liability and as Director of Communications it is my duty to warn you of what I see as the likely public reaction.

ARTHUR: I'm afraid I disagree. He has been vital in the election campaign. He is someone who has overcome adversity.

LAWRENCE enters.

ARTHUR: Lawrence, as you see we are debating the strengths of our new cabinet.

LAWRENCE: I am delighted that I am to be given the opportunity to serve, sir

ARTHUR: I was just discussing your background, with Morgan.

LAWRENCE: I can see that I might not be to everyone's taste.

MORGAN: Did you get that from one of your focus groups?

LAWRENCE: An internal memo, unsigned.

ARTHUR: Gentlemen, please, this is a moment of history. What we are about to create will last. We will all have to make judgements, sacrifices. This is the moment for the party. Are you going to accept the challenge?

LAWRENCE: I have prepared my opening statement.

ARTHUR: Morgan?

MORGAN: Of course, sir.

ARTHUR: Then it is time to face the people.

Lights and camera flashes. Projection and music. Time passing.

LAWRENCE takes the role of a Government Minister. ARTHUR, GWEN and MORGAN take the role of reporters.

REPORTER 1: Minister, how do you answer the charge that by giving away our currency you are giving away our heritage?

LAWRENCE: We have always been a pragmatic people. It is now time for a change to embrace the future.

REPORTER 2: Minister, the health service is one of our national institutions, are you right to undermine its strength with direct service private hospitals?

LAWRENCE: The new schemes will allow people to make real contributions to the decisions that effect their health.

REPORTER 3: Are we not right to fear control by the state where a country legislates to record all its citizens by shades in their irises?

MORGAN takes the camera and films LAWRENCE, projecting his image on screen.

LAWRENCE: The introduction of a national identity card will ensure that only people that are properly entitled to the benefits and advantages of living in this country will receive them. People who have contributed, people who pay taxes. Our people.

LAWRENCE turns around to view his last image on the screen. GWEN and ARTHUR take up positions within the cabinet room. LAWRENCE walks away from the centre of the discussion. His image remains on the screen.

MORGAN: The ratings have improved.

ARTHUR: How much?

MORGAN: Enough. We are not at risk.

GWEN: We should have stuck to our promises.

MORGAN: We couldn't afford to.

GWEN: We came to power to make changes, not compromises.

ARTHUR: This way we will still get the changes we need.

GWEN: Eighteen months into power and we have to put D'Lac in front of the cameras?

MORGAN: Lawrence is very good at presenting a united front on issues that threaten to split the party.

ARTHUR: Maybe I should take the weekly press conference?

MORGAN: As leader you should not over expose yourself to questions.

GWEN: I think we are relying too much on Lawrence.

MORGAN: He has proved himself very adept at answering questions.

GWEN: Not necessarily the ones that were asked.

MORGAN: That is not exactly a criticism.

GWEN: We need something more than good presentation.

MORGAN: I cannot present promises.

GWEN: Exactly, that is why we need to stick to the manifesto.

ARTHUR: Over the long term our approval rating has been falling. The people are getting a bit restless now the honeymoon period is over.

GWEN: I was hoping it might have lasted a bit longer.

MORGAN: We need to put the caring side of the party back in people's minds. Remind them that we are human, just like them.

ARTHUR: Excellent, any ideas.

MORGAN: We've had a request from Victor Doyle to appear on his programme.

ARTHUR: Victor Doyle?

MORGAN: He hosts a chat show on Friday night, live.

ARTHUR: I have seen it.

LAWRENCE enters.

ARTHUR: What do you think, Lawrence – Victor Doyle?

LAWRENCE: He's a second-rate quiz show contestant who got lucky.

MORGAN: With very high audience figures.

ARTHUR: Surely you're not seriously suggesting that I appear on his programme? Shall I take my trombone along, as well?

MORGAN: No, of course not. He very much wants to interview the First Lady.

LAWRENCE: He should be told to keep to the desperate celebrities he usually invites.

MORGAN: Along with the occasional guest of stature and integrity.

LAWRENCE: Like who?

GWEN: He did interview the new Archbishop a few months ago.

LAWRENCE: And what will exposing the First Lady to the charms of Mr Doyle help us to achieve?

MORGAN: It will help us appear as a party with a leader and his wife in touch with the people.

LAWRENCE: I cannot believe you are taking this request seriously.

MORGAN: It can do us no harm. The people do not always want bad news from politicians.

GWEN: I would welcome some light entertainment.

ARTHUR: I might even watch the show.

LAWRENCE: We should not expose ourselves to the pointless cabaret of a gossip show.

GWEN: It might be a bit of fun. No one takes these things too seriously.

ARTHUR: We can agree the questions beforehand.

LAWRENCE: In my opinion a live show with a late night audience is not the best place to profile the First Lady.

GWEN: I'm sure I can handle myself with Victor Doyle.

Music. Projection: 'The Victor Doyle Experience'.

ARTHUR, LAWRENCE and GWEN retreat to the shadows. MORGAN takes the role of VICTOR DOYLE. He puts on a tasteless, orange jacket and a red wig. He gets up and accepts the applause of the audience.

217

Projection: 'Applause'.

VICTOR: It's 'The Victor Doyle Experience'. And aren't you lucky to catch it? Tonight, I'm showing my serious side. Down with soap actresses who just want to promote their books; down with second-rate comedians who just want to promote their TV shows. Tonight, Victor Doyle is getting really serious; Victor Doyle is getting down with the most important woman in the country. Ladies and gentlemen, because it is Friday night after all, please welcome our beloved First Lady. The witty, the wicked, the wonderful, Gwen Lloyd.

Lights flash as GWEN enters. She is overwhelmed by the introduction and the reception. She is not used to the ambience of 'The Victor Doyle Experience'.

VICTOR: I must say it is such a pleasure to have someone of stature on my show, at last. Apart from me, that is. Tell me, Gwen, can I call you Gwen? Good. I like to start on first-name terms. It's when they sue me, they call me Mr Doyle. You can call me Victor. We would have invited your husband but he's an incredibly busy man and we wanted someone with more insight into a politician's life. Someone who has to wash his socks in the morning. And, hopefully, his back at night.

GWEN: It's a pleasure to be here, Victor.

VICTOR: Of course. They all say that.

GWEN: But I mean it.

VICTOR: Oh, isn't she sweet, ladies and gentlemen. Enough to eat.... So tell me, can you remember the first time you met? Staring across the university quad, boating on the river, your eyes locked and the bells started ringing.

GWEN: No, we met in a political meeting.

VICTOR: No romance there, then. But there must have been fire stirring because within six months you were married. Don't you think you rushed into things a bit? A bit like the present Government?

GWEN: When you feel you're right for someone, there's no point in waiting.

VICTOR: So, wedding bells, where did he take you on honeymoon? Did the earth move?

GWEN: We went to Provence.

VICTOR: What a romantic destination. I always loved Spain. Bullfights, sangria, men in tight trousers. And you've been in love ever since?

GWEN: Of course.

VICTOR: Isn't power meant to be one of the great aphrodisiacs?

GWEN: We have a very strong relationship. We are committed to each other and the cause of the party and the country.

VICTOR: But doesn't all that world politics sometimes get in the way of love? Don't you wish that the world would just leave you alone for a few hours so you can have your man to yourself?

GWEN: When we married I realised Arthur was a man of commitment. He had certain goals, things he wanted to do with his life to make things better for other people. I shared those aspirations.

VICTOR (*to GWEN, only*): But this is friday night and they just want a laugh. (*To audience:*) Tell us about some of the other members of that kitchen cabinet.

GWEN: We all get on very well.

VICTOR: Lawrence, he's a bit of alright isn't he?

GWEN: We all have our own roles to play. Lawrence is making a fine contribution as First Minister.

VICTOR: He's finding his way around at night?

GWEN: What do you mean?

VICTOR: You know what they say about the Greeks.

GWEN: I believe his family is from France.

VICTOR: Yes, well.... And Morgan, I've heard he's a man of many talents?

GWEN: Morgan has been a faithful supporter.

VICTOR: Isn't that political talk for we're about to get rid of him?

GWEN: You're terribly cynical.

VICTOR: Oh I am, aren't we all. It comes from working here for so long. Turn around and someone will put a knife in you. I've got to be constantly on my guard or younger better looking men will take my place. But I'm sure you know all about that.

GWEN: No, not yet.

VICTOR: I see…. So you're a couple that puts work in front of everything else?

GWEN: We often try to combine work with pleasure.

VICTOR: I try to combine pleasure with pleasure myself, but each to his own. But what about a real holiday? I remember you looking so romantic together in front of the pyramids in India.

GWEN: It was the Taj Mahal.

VICTOR: Of course it was darling. It's my favourite Indian restaurant. Everything with spice, just like me.

GWEN: I can imagine.

VICTOR: A born politician, ladies and gentlemen. Isn't she lovely but before we let her go back to the bedrooms of power, the old Victor Doyle tradition of a duet. And I know she wasn't expecting this but we've done our research and discovered she's the cabaret star at party fund-raising nights. So what do you say?

GWEN: I'm not sure… I thought we agreed not to sing.

VICTOR: Of course we did but I won't take no as an answer.

VICTOR takes her hand and pulls her up before the audience. She shuffles nervously, before launching into the first bars of a song – Frank Sinatra's 'Something Stupid'. The lights isolate her. She begins to sing – and sing well – a duet with VICTOR. The lyrics are projected on screen, as a karaoke number. The lights fade.

It is a debrief meeting. No one wants to speak first. GWEN is furious. MORGAN returns. He waits for her to speak.

GWEN: I was totally humiliated.

MORGAN: I thought you sang rather well.

GWEN: Victor Doyle had twenty minutes of fun with our life. To what end?

MORGAN: The press reports are... reasonably positive.

GWEN: I should have listened to the First Minister. At least he had my best interests at heart.

ARTHUR: You were rather keen to appear?

GWEN: Not to humiliate myself.

MORGAN: I'm afraid public situations cannot always be controlled.

LAWRENCE enters.

MORGAN: The knight errant.

ARTHUR: Did you see the show, Lawrence?

LAWRENCE: I was at a fringe meeting but I've seen a recording.... I don't think the First Lady should have been exposed to such an unpredictable live performance.

MORGAN: Are you the Director of Communications now?

GWEN: What happened to the agreed questions about my constituency work and the charitable trusts we've set up?

MORGAN: Mr Doyle ignored the prepared questions.

LAWRENCE: He never sticks to the script, it's one of the features about the show.

GWEN: He was only interested in our love life.

ARTHUR: Yes... quite.

LAWRENCE: I think such public exhibitions are best left to the professionals who need the publicity... and the one thing we don't need is more publicity.

ARTHUR: Perhaps a degree of respectable distance is called for?

MORGAN: I will chair an enquiry of the whole process, sir.

ARTHUR: Good. Please get it done as soon as possible.

MORGAN: Absolutely.

ARTHUR: I hope so.

MORGAN leaves.

ARTHUR: Yes, Lawrence?

LAWRENCE: There is some matter I need to discuss, sir.

ARTHUR: And?

LAWRENCE: It is of a highly sensitive nature.

ARTHUR: Is it political?

LAWRENCE looks at GWEN.

LAWRENCE: Yes.

ARTHUR: Then my wife is perfectly capable of joining the conversation.

LAWRENCE: Of course, sir.

ARTHUR: Well?

LAWRENCE: There's news of further difficulty in the Levant. It will require your immediate attention. Our envoi needs to speak to you.

ARTHUR: Really, now?

LAWRENCE: It would be best, sir.

ARTHUR: Very well, I will join you in a moment.

LAWRENCE: Thank you, sir.

LAWRENCE leaves.

ARTHUR: I'm sorry, Gwen.

GWEN: It's gone now. No one will remember it in a few weeks.

ARTHUR: But I should have thought it through.

GWEN: It was free entertainment for the masses.

ARTHUR: That is Victor Doyle's role.

GWEN: I rather enjoyed the singing.

ARTHUR: I always loved your singing.

GWEN: Really?

ARTHUR: You know I do.

GWEN: You haven't told me lately. I feel the work is everything now. When we were planning all this, just us, in our own flat, we had each other and a few ideas. I loved those times, Arthur.

ARTHUR: They haven't gone, Gwen.

GWEN: They are yesterday, the past is always that. Sometimes you are happy, sometimes sad but it is always the past.

ARTHUR: We are the same people.

GWEN: How can we be? Look at us, we have staff, a private car, flights to meet the leaders of countries I was only a tourist in ten years ago.

ARTHUR: The standard of accommodation has improved.

GWEN: And what do we see?

ARTHUR: I rather enjoyed the Taj Mahal without the people.

GWEN: They kept everybody else out for the day.

ARTHUR: And we could see the architecture.

GWEN: Yes, walk around an old tomb on our own. The king built Taj Mahal because he missed his wife. I miss being with Arthur Lloyd. Just you, not the President and his men.

ARTHUR: It has been a difficult year. I'm sorry if I have been distracted. I will try to make some more time just for us. Shall we go to France this summer?

GWEN: Really?

ARTHUR: Of course.

GWEN: Just us?

ARTHUR: I don't think it will be just us.

GWEN: No meetings then?

ARTHUR: Just a holiday in France.

GWEN: Will it be wise, politically?

ARTHUR: You can't always live by what will be wise for the electorate.

GWEN: Are you sure about that?

GWEN kisses ARTHUR.

The lights fade. ARTHUR is, again, isolated on the stage. Lights flash. He takes up his position, centre stage, to field questions.

ARTHUR: I am fully aware of the implications of such a position.

REPORTER 1: Is the President aware of the public reaction to revelations of his private life on a late night television show?

ARTHUR: I'm sure the people will be able to make their own judgments on the value of such knowledge.

REPORTER 4: Do you think it was a wise decision to sanction such a public performance, with your approval rating already falling?

ARTHUR: We consider all requests for interviews and public appearances. My approval rating is always under scrutiny. I try to perform my role to the best of my ability and let the public judge from the results.

REPORTER 4: How do you answer the charge that your administration is obsessed with image rather than content?

ARTHUR: We put forward our policies in the best possible light because we think they will work for the country and the people.

REPORTER 1: Is it true that you will be sponsoring a new theme show looking for talented ministers to perform in public?

ARTHUR: With the current and ongoing crisis in the Levant, I would have thought my ministers will have enough to concentrate on. Thank you. I really must close. *(He leaves them still asking questions.)*

REPORTER 4: Mr President, how do you respond to charges of rivalry between your ministers?

REPORTER 1: Mr President, how do you consider your strength of support within the party?

REPORTER 4: Mr President, will there be further opportunities for junior ministers ?

REPORTER 1: Mr President...

REPORTER 4: Mr President.

They take off their hats. Music. Time passing.

LAWRENCE: I do not agree.

MORGAN: It is not your decision.

LAWRENCE: For him to leave the country at this time would be a grave mistake.

MORGAN: It is imperative that he is seen to take on a more positive role abroad.

LAWRENCE: We have domestic issues to contend with.

MORGAN: Our national security is at stake. His influence in the crisis may be crucial.

LAWRENCE: The Levant issue is beyond our control.

MORGAN: But not our influence. When the situation settles down we will be in a better position to take advantage of the opportunities.

LAWRENCE: It is not a good enough reason for Arthur to travel abroad at this time. The party is becoming restless for progress on our manifesto. It has been two years.

MORGAN: May I remind you that domestic issues are the responsibility of the First Minister who needs to report to the President. Are you saying that you will be unable to keep the country and the party in line during a brief overseas engagement?

LAWRENCE: There is a perception that the President is spending too much time on foreign policy issues and neglecting the people who elected him.

MORGAN: And it is my decision that a short overseas diplomatic mission will increase the public's perception of Arthur as a man within the wider world context.

LAWRENCE: And if we are isolated by events?

MORGAN: We cannot protect Arthur from events.

LAWRENCE: But we are in a position where we must put the country first.

MORGAN: That is exactly what I am doing.

LAWRENCE: I see the mission as a mistake. We will be exposed.

MORGAN: Arthur is a fine man and a good leader but he is not the country. Time will produce other leaders and other opportunities.

LAWRENCE: In a democracy it is for the people to decide.

MORGAN: The people will have the right choice when the time comes.

LAWRENCE: There is only one man to lead this party into the future.

ARTHUR enters.

ARTHUR: I see my impending journey is providing more cause for argument.

MORGAN: We were just discussing the necessity of this short visit abroad.

ARTHUR: Precisely, my wife also has her concerns but I have tried to allay them. She tells me it is not a good time to leave. What do you say, Lawrence?

LAWRENCE: The decision needs to be made with some caution.

ARTHUR: No, with confidence. It is not always a good time to leave but at least then I will have the pleasure of a homecoming. Gentlemen, we need to prepare. Morgan, is the briefing paper ready?

MORGAN: Yes, it is in my office.

ARTHUR: And the press conference?

MORGAN: I have called a meeting for five. It will give them enough time to edit it for the evening news.

ARTHUR: Excellent. Flights?

MORGAN: First thing tomorrow.

ARTHUR: Then we must hurry. Lawrence, we need to talk later, there are some party issues I need to discuss.

ARTHUR and MORGAN leave. GWEN enters.

GWEN: You seem concerned?

LAWRENCE: This mission is unnecessary.

GWEN: What would you suggest?

LAWRENCE: There are issues here.

GWEN: There are always concerns at home.

LAWRENCE: Then perhaps it is always better to stay at home.

GWEN: Arthur wants to make a difference in the world. I am more concerned about some of Morgan's methods.

LAWRENCE: He has an unconventional approach.

GWEN: He exposes Arthur to too much pressure.

LAWRENCE: He thinks he can control the press but it is not always the case.

GWEN: Are you going to stop him going?

LAWRENCE: He knows my advice.

GWEN: You are just going to let this happen?

LAWRENCE: Arthur is his own man in the end.

GWEN: He has been appreciative of your support. In this world there are always people who will undermine him.

LAWRENCE: I am grateful for the opportunities he has provided for me.

GWEN: He thinks highly of you. We both do.

LAWRENCE: Yes, I will try to do my best for you both.

GWEN looks at LAWRENCE.

LAWRENCE: I must go. There is always business to attend to.

GWEN: Always....

Music. Time passes. ARTHUR enters, to flashlights. He is projected onto the screen. He is alone, against the press conference.

ARTHUR: It would be wrong of a leader at this time to ignore the realities of such a world. We are faced with threats that oppose our way of life and the freedoms we hold dear. It is as an advocate of these freedoms that I have decided at this time to embark upon this mission. We need to make a difference. This is the opportunity. To do nothing is not an option.

REPORTER 4: What is the President's reaction to criticism of the administration in ignoring pressing domestic issues while concentrating on world affairs?

ARTHUR: We are a team. I would not be able to secure our position abroad if I wasn't totally confident of the ability and loyalty of our people at home.

REPORTER 1: Is there any truth in the suggestion that certain members of your own party consider your leadership to be under threat?

ARTHUR: My role is always under constant discussion both at home and abroad. It comes with the position. Thank you for your time. (*He leaves.*)

Projection, music. The lights cut. The image of ARTHUR is left on the screen.

The REPORTERS leave. ARTHUR retreats. GWEN enters. She runs a projection. It reveals a montage of images framing her life with Arthur; a short expressionistic film that begins to fragment at the edges. She is absorbed in the memories. LAWRENCE enters.

233

LAWRENCE: I'm sorry, I didn't mean to disturb you.

GWEN: Not at all, I was just... looking back.

LAWRENCE: Good memories?

GWEN: Of course.

LAWRENCE: You looked young, happy?

GWEN: They seem a long time ago.

LAWRENCE: You haven't changed.

GWEN: No... but it was much simpler then, that's all.

LAWRENCE: As we get older time moves faster.

GWEN: You are young to be looking that far back, Lawrence.

LAWRENCE: It is too easy to see into the past.

GWEN: Understand it backwards, live it forwards?

LAWRENCE: I'm looking for Arthur?

GWEN: He's not here.

LAWRENCE: I see....

GWEN: Can I help?

LAWRENCE: We have a problem with the party.... I don't think so.

GWEN: There was a time when the party welcomed my input.

LAWRENCE: It is not something I should discuss with anyone but Arthur.

GWEN: Of course. I am a good influence on his wardrobe.

LAWRENCE: You underestimate your role.

GWEN: I wanted to be a politician.

LAWRENCE: You are part of the process.

GWEN: You really think so?

LAWRENCE: Absolutely... you have real influence.

GWEN: Then you are listening to our own press releases.

LAWRENCE: I try to maintain a balanced opinion.

GWEN: We all have to do that.

LAWRENCE: You are important. Arthur is aware of your... value.

GWEN: Lawrence, please stop talking to me as if I'm interviewing you.

LAWRENCE: Sorry, I was trying to be diplomatic.

GWEN: What for?

LAWRENCE: It's a way of avoiding what I want to say.

GWEN: That's better. Now you are speaking to me. What do you want to say?

LAWRENCE: I'd rather not say.

GWEN: Here we go again.

LAWRENCE: Some things are better not said.

GWEN: Lawrence, could you ever be spontaneous?

LAWRENCE: I'd have to think about it.

GWEN: You should allow yourself to be guided by your feelings rather than just your intellect.

LAWRENCE: I will try to consider it.

GWEN: I like you, Lawrence.

LAWRENCE: Thank you.

GWEN: I didn't used to. I used to think you were humourless, boring, totally one track mind work obsessed.

LAWRENCE: That's quite a list.

GWEN: It was just a start.

LAWRENCE: And now?

GWEN: Now, I just like you....

LAWRENCE and GWEN have a moment of realisation, of mutual attraction. They are both rather surprised and nervous.

ARTHUR enters. LAWRENCE rushes to defend himself against charges that have not been made. ARTHUR is cautious.

ARTHUR: A court in my absence?

LAWRENCE: We were just discussing the political situation. The First Lady had some interesting ideas.

ARTHUR: Of course, she is a born politician.

GWEN: I was making a few suggestions for the mission.

ARTHUR: We need to take as many opinions as possible. You never know when they become useful.

LAWRENCE: I called to give my apologies regarding our dinner appointment.

ARTHUR: You will not be joining us?

LAWRENCE: I'm afraid there's some urgent business in the north. I must attend to it.

ARTHUR: What is it?

LAWRENCE: It might be nothing but I need to talk to a few of the community leaders to settle matters.

ARTHUR: Do you intend to remain there long?

LAWRENCE: No, I will return tomorrow evening at the latest.

ARTHUR: Good. I do not think it is good for you to be out of the capital for too long while I'm away. The press won't like it.

LAWRENCE: I've arranged for a couple of photocalls tomorrow. It should give us some excellent editorial.

ARTHUR: Good. Nothing too positive without me you understand.

LAWRENCE: No, of course... please, you must excuse me. I need to make the last train connection. (*He leaves.*)

GWEN looks at ARTHUR.

ARTHUR: Only having a bit of fun. His earnestness needs to be lightened sometimes.

GWEN: I find it rather endearing.

ARTHUR: You didn't like him a year ago.

GWEN: I thought he was a bit too polished.

ARTHUR: And now he's not?

GWEN: We've got to know him. He doesn't think you should go, either.

ARTHUR: I know. I've read his briefing paper.

GWEN: Then why leave now?

ARTHUR: I'm committed to it. If I cancel a mission because of a little domestic difficulty how will I be perceived in the world?

GWEN: What about home? Our French holiday?

ARTHUR: You know I've cleared some time in the autumn.

GWEN: It won't be the same.

ARTHUR: Provence is beautiful in December.

GWEN: It rains in December.

ARTHUR: It will be just us. I promise.

GWEN: You promised already.

ARTHUR: I've got to react to events, remain flexible. This is important for us.

GWEN: Yes, it is.

ARTHUR: I cannot help the situation.

GWEN: Neither can I.

ARTHUR: Gwen, please, we've one more night. I don't want to spend it arguing.

GWEN: I'm sorry. I'm tired as well.

ARTHUR: I want us to be together on this.

GWEN: I know.

ARTHUR: I want the best for us both.

GWEN: Are you sure?

ARTHUR: Of course.

GWEN: Then don't go.

ARTHUR: I cannot pull back.

GWEN Leaves. Lights fade.

LAWRENCE (*enters and approaches the podium*): We live in good times, let us not now sour them with enmity and discord but let us cement friendships with peace and goodwill.

MORGAN films LAWRENCE. The image is projected on screen. MORGAN edits the words down to:

LAWRENCE (*on screen*): Let us cement friendships with peace and goodwill.

MORGAN edits, again.

LAWRENCE (*on screen*): Let us have friendship with peace.

MORGAN edits, again.

Projection: 'News Flash' in big letters.

LAWRENCE (*on screen*): This school that I have officially opened this afternoon is not just a new school but a new start, a new future.

Projection: 'News Flash' in big letters.

LAWRENCE (*on screen*): It is through all our hard work that we are able to invest in this shining example of new health care in a new age.

Projection: 'News Flash' in big letters.

LAWRENCE (*on screen*): This isn't just new investment. It is our future.

LAWRENCE holds the stare of the cameras. His image leaves the screen, which cuts to black.

Time has passed.

LAWRENCE: Things have changed... in the country.

GWEN: You have handled the situation very well.

LAWRENCE: I am a politician. It is my job.

GWEN: People have seen an unexpected side of you.

LAWRENCE: Gwen, you asked me to express my feelings.

GWEN: I thought you should be more in touch with yourself. Allow yourself more freedom.

LAWRENCE: I have done that in my work.

GWEN: Then it has been a success.

LAWRENCE: But not until now with my life.

GWEN: We will all go along as before. It is only a matter of time before he returns.

LAWRENCE: I am not sure where the future is taking us.

GWEN: I have a role.

LAWRENCE: Gwen, I'm falling in love with you.

GWEN: How can you be? I am another man's wife.

LAWRENCE: And I am a man. A man with desires and needs. I have never had love in my life before you.

GWEN: And do you believe this is love?

LAWRENCE: It is not always helpful to believe in things. Sometimes it is enough just to act.

LAWRENCE moves towards GWEN. He takes her head in his hands. The screen flickers into a shadowy figure watching them. It is MORGAN. They do not notice.

GWEN: You do not know what you do?

GWEN kisses LAWRENCE. The lights fade.

MORGAN is on screen, watching them. The screen cuts.

ACT TWO

The stage is darker, reflecting the changed times. LAWRENCE and GWEN share a slow dance – an echo of her dance with Arthur. Arthur's image appears on screen. LAWRENCE is left, watching.

ARTHUR: It has been a rewarding mission. We have spoken to many people, listened to opinions, tried to broaden our perspectives.... I feel that in bringing the issues into the open, we have helped broker this fragile but welcome peace.

MORGAN enters. He freezes Arthur's image. MORGAN and LAWRENCE assess each other.

MORGAN: Are the allegations true?

LAWRENCE: They will not be able to print anything.

MORGAN: Why not?

LAWRENCE: I've checked the legal situation. We can shut them down.

MORGAN: What for?

LAWRENCE: Printing lies.

MORGAN: You don't realise the danger we're in if even a rumour gets to the wrong people.

LAWRENCE: And who would they be?

MORGAN: We are a party that needs to be seen above such scandal.

LAWRENCE: I have said they are lies. Are you doubting me?

MORGAN: I am aware of what the truth could mean.

LAWRENCE: Then you must take your concerns to the President.

MORGAN: You are sure there is no substance to these stories?

LAWRENCE: Your job is to control the press. Are you able to do it?

MORGAN: I need to know if there is any truth in the story?

GWEN enters.

GWEN: I did not know we had a press briefing today?

MORGAN: I'm sorry?

GWEN: My office is getting requests for an interview.

MORGAN: There are some concerns that are not being met by the usual channels.

GWEN: You know I cannot be subjected to press speculation.

MORGAN: Madam, we were just discussing some concerns...

LAWRENCE: Regarding how well the Director of Communications can do his job. Morgan was just leaving.

MORGAN assesses his position and leaves.

LAWRENCE: He is returning in the morning.

GWEN: The mission has been a success.

LAWRENCE: He has proved himself an able statesman.

GWEN: You thought it would fail?

LAWRENCE: I think it had challenges. He has met them.

GWEN: What have we done, Lawrence?

LAWRENCE: We have done what people do.

GWEN: And now?

LAWRENCE: We return to our past.

GWEN: I can't just go on as before. I have changed.

LAWRENCE: I know. We have both changed. I can't explain it... but there are realities. You are a married woman, Arthur is someone who I respect. What are these words? They mean nothing. They are just words with which I have already protected myself...

GWEN: Why are you saying this?

LAWRENCE: We have to forget it. For Arthur. He will need our support.

GWEN: You cannot just leave things go.

LAWRENCE: I acted and now I must deal with the consequences.

GWEN: Where does that leave me? Us? Lawrence, I love you.

LAWRENCE: We have to return to our past.

GWEN: No, it is no use. It is another country.

LAWRENCE: Gwen, please. I have to prepare....

GWEN leaves. LAWRENCE is left with the darkness.

MORGAN appears on a common, at night. KELLY enters. She is dressed as a modern Newsnight reporter, in a sharp suit.

KELLY: Hell, Morgan, this is a forsaken place. Couldn't we have met in town? Inside? In the dry? This is my best suit.

MORGAN: You've never been a good dresser. Anyway I would have been recognised in the places you work out of.

KELLY: I wouldn't be so sure. One face is as good as the next. I've seen a few out on the common. They're not your type.

MORGAN: And how would you know my tastes?

KELLY (*looking him up and down*): Yeh, maybe you're right. So what's the news?

MORGAN: We're visiting the estate tomorrow. I thought there might be a story in it for you.

KELLY: Of course there is, the beneficence of Arthur. We get a weekly press release on his goodness, consideration and even, recently, wit.

MORGAN: I might be able to provide some local colour for you?

KELLY: Depends what I've got to do for it.

MORGAN: I'd like it covered with your usual journalistic integrity.

KELLY: And you have a new idea... sorry, policy initiative?

MORGAN: Arthur's had a few petitions for help and we want to be seen to be doing something.

KELLY: What's the cause this time?

MORGAN: Family stability. It's a great concern of the party. We need to be shoring up the country, setting an example.

KELLY: The caring face of Arthur?

MORGAN: It is time for a change of focus. We... Arthur feels it's time to concentrate on the issues at home.

KELLY: There's a lot of air here, Morgan, where's the motive?

MORGAN: I give you the details, you write the story.

KELLY: There is no story, this is rubbish. It's the same press release, where's the spin? I'm a professional you know.

MORGAN: We want to be seen to be supportive, especially in the estates.

KELLY: You're worried about publicity from people who don't count?

MORGAN: We are concerned with the state of the country.

KELLY: Of course, that's in your job description. Mine is to write news.

MORGAN: You can do that?

KELLY: Not with this.

MORGAN: That's all I have.

KELLY: Forget it then.

MORGAN: You run this and I'll give you the first take on a story that will keep you in designer wear for a year.

KELLY: That's a lot of clothes.

MORGAN: Can you trust me?

KELLY: Hell, no but I might be interested in a gamble. So the rumours are true then?

MORGAN: You will not be able to print it yet.

KELLY: We are checking the legal situation now.

MORGAN: We don't want the information in the wrong hands at the wrong time.

KELLY: It is of public interest.

MORGAN: I don't care if it's in the public interest it will not be in your interest?

KELLY: Are you trying to restrict press freedoms?

MORGAN: I think you understand the position.

KELLY: Give me the story then. I'll make it in your interest.

MORGAN: Relationships are a key feature of the regime just now. I find political marriages always come with an air of compromise.

KELLY: And is there anyone particular being compromised?

MORGAN: Come, Kelly. I don't want to write the story for you. I'm just saying there's one there. Arthur has spent a lot of time out of the country. The First Lady has found some time to pursue her own party interests. The First Minister has always been helpful in supporting the best interests of the party. He has proved himself very amenable this time.

KELLY: I'll need some proof.

MORGAN: There'll be more. As time goes on.

KELLY: I hope you know I'll be doing you a favour.

MORGAN: Of course.

KELLY: I guess I'll be going then. Don't suppose you fancy a drink?

MORGAN: I thought I might stay around here. There may be some further opportunities.

KELLY: Aye, well make sure you don't get caught. 'Cause if you do, I'll enjoy ruining your career.

MORGAN: You'll have no need to do that.

KELLY leaves.

MORGAN takes off his coat. They return to the cabinet room. ARTHUR returns to the atrium. MORGAN brings in a large pile of papers. He places them on the desk.

ARTHUR: More problems from the press?

MORGAN: Some concerns.

ARTHUR: Our mission has been well received.

MORGAN: They have already forgotten about the Levant. They want our reaction to the trouble in the north.

ARTHUR: We should set up a select committee to look into the affair.

MORGAN: I wish we didn't have to undergo this pretence of democracy every time something goes wrong.

ARTHUR: It is necessary not just to be listening to the people but to be seen to be listening. Can we ask Lawrence to chair it?

MORGAN: Lawrence has been involved with his own projects. He was very active during your time away.

ARTHUR: I have seen some of the reports. The coverage of the estates initiative was very positive.

MORGAN: He has many admirers but we need to be wary of his new found popularity. His press appearances tend to be very effective with some of the people. But a certain sort of people. Not necessarily our people.

ARTHUR: Are you suggesting Lawrence's success comes with other motives?

MORGAN: Some people in the party see him as a man with a future. They are jealous of his intimacy within your inner circle.

ARTHUR: I have given him opportunity, that is all.

MORGAN: You are seen to forgive all his faults. He has made a few mistakes. You have ignored them.

ARTHUR: No one is above making a mistake. I am rewarding his loyalty. I also see him as a man with a future.

MORGAN: He is close to the First Lady. You ignore it.

ARTHUR: What exactly are you saying, Morgan?

MORGAN: He is someone that you forgive easily. Even overlook actions.

ARTHUR: Does this directly concern the First Lady?

MORGAN: He is close to her.

ARTHUR: And?

MORGAN: They have a friendship.

ARTHUR: And that is all, Morgan.

MORGAN: Some would see it as inappropriate.

ARTHUR: Would you?

MORGAN: It is not my business, directly.

ARTHUR: But you are advising me of it. What are you suggesting?

MORGAN: That their friendship is more than just... that it is dangerous for you.

ARTHUR: Morgan, I need you to retract that statement.

GWEN enters.

GWEN: Problems gentlemen?

ARTHUR: Always something to discuss.

GWEN: Shall I do another song for Victor Doyle?

MORGAN: I don't think that sacrifice will be necessary.

ARTHUR: We need to move forward with our domestic policy. The Levant was a necessary and successful mission but that time is over. Are we prepared for the press conference?

MORGAN: I'm in the process of drafting a statement.

ARTHUR: Good, shall we meet in an hour to discuss the details?

MORGAN: Certainly, sir. (*He leaves.*)

ARTHUR: It is good to be back, Gwen.

GWEN: You have been missed.

ARTHUR: I would like to think so.

GWEN: It has not been the same without you.

ARTHUR: Come, surely you were able to make use of the time?

GWEN: I was distracted. It has been difficult here without you.

ARTHUR: I hear Lawrence has been supportive...

GWEN: The people seem to like him.

ARTHUR: And you?

GWEN: Of course.

ARTHUR: Good, yes, he has been a fine minister.

GWEN: I don't think Morgan likes him very much.

ARTHUR: You used to find him humourless?

GWEN: I didn't know him.

ARTHUR: Morgan is jealous of his easy charm with the media.

GWEN: So what way for us, now?

ARTHUR: Same as always. What else are we to do?

GWEN: I was wondering about our holiday?

ARTHUR: Of course, France...

GWEN: I think we need to spend some more time together.

ARTHUR: Of course...

GWEN: We need to talk.

ARTHUR: Yes, and drink fine champagne.

GWEN: About our future beyond this party?

ARTHUR: I don't think we can afford to think too far ahead.

GWEN: It is not so far.

ARTHUR: The elections are due. We will need to be seen providing a united front.

GWEN: Yes, the election campaign.

ARTHUR: I detect some reluctance?

GWEN: I am tired of the scrutiny. All those pointless questions.

ARTHUR: And are we able to face these questions?

GWEN: You have been very successful.

ARTHUR: And what of us?

GWEN: It is not us, Arthur. It is me.

ARTHUR: Yes.

GWEN: I... I have not been the woman you need me to be.

ARTHUR: Of course you have.

GWEN: You need someone who supports you. I make mistakes. I can't live in this world of scrutiny with you anymore.

ARTHUR: Gwen, please. Do not upset yourself. We can come through this. Whatever it is I will understand. You do not need to tell me. (*He leaves.*)

Lights flash. MORGAN films ARTHUR on the podium. The press appear. They have lost their tone of respect for the leader. They bait him.

REPORTER 2: There is speculation concerning the public role of your wife?

REPORTER 4: What is the state of your marriage?

REPORTER 2: Are the First Lady and the First Minister having an affair?

ARTHUR is silent.

MORGAN (*addressing the TV audience*): The President is only able to accept questions directly relating to his press statement. Thank you for your patience.

ARTHUR: I would like to take this opportunity to reflect on recent events.... (*Fades out, to silence.*)

The lights fade on the screen and ARTHUR.

MORGAN and ARTHUR move to the cabinet room.

MORGAN: Don't worry yet. I will be able to build on this.

ARTHUR: What were you doing calling an end to the conference?

MORGAN: It was embarrassing.

ARTHUR: For whom?

MORGAN: The country.

ARTHUR: And are you a judge of the country?

MORGAN: I see a man I respect, ridiculed.

ARTHUR: I am Arthur.

MORGAN: Then you are undone by your own foolishness. They, the people you love, have made fools of you.

ARTHUR: How dare you talk about them like that.

MORGAN: Do you believe they are honourable?

ARTHUR: I do not blame them.

MORGAN: Who do you blame, then?

ARTHUR (*looks into himself*): You cannot help me in this Morgan. You need to allow me to face it alone.

MORGAN: My resignation will be with you tonight.

The screen flickers into life. Fragments of Arthur's speech are projected: 'I feel it a leaders duty... now the time to explain... their own conclusions... reflected our desire...'. The projection varies between silence and a distorted picture. MORGAN is orchestrating a disintegration of Arthur's image. ARTHUR is increasingly concerned by his lack of sound and presentation. The sound returns in bites, then the picture. Lights cut and flash. MORGAN leaves.

ARTHUR is alone. LAWRENCE enters the atrium. ARTHUR waits for him to speak. LAWRENCE is waiting to be spoken to.

ARTHUR: It is a difficult time, Lawrence.

LAWRENCE: I watched the press conference. I thought you handled the presentation difficulties well.

ARTHUR: They just wait for us out there, the wolves. Wait for a slip, a sleight of hand.

LAWRENCE: The administration is still strong.

ARTHUR: I do not think so.

LAWRENCE: The reforms we have implemented will soon be working.

ARTHUR: But will they be seen to be working? People need more than figures, they want the future.

LAWRENCE: And it will come.

ARTHUR: Yes, but not for me.

LAWRENCE: Then I should also resign.

ARTHUR: Why?

LAWRENCE: I am provoking much speculation.

ARTHUR: You are seen as a popular man. Everyone in the country loves you.

LAWRENCE: I did not seek popularity. I wanted to be part of the project we put forward.

ARTHUR: Then why the resignation?

LAWRENCE: I think you will find it hard to understand.

ARTHUR: And it's rubbish, Lawrence. You should know the press need something to talk about. I was away. You went to dinner with my wife. So what?

LAWRENCE: I wasn't aware of the difficulties it would cause.

ARTHUR: Of course not.

LAWRENCE: I was naive in my presumption that I could control the media speculation of such actions.

ARTHUR: Press control was Morgan's responsibility and he has spectacularly failed in that.

LAWRENCE: Still I feel it is my duty at this time to show some honour and resign my position.

ARTHUR: Lawrence, I do not have many friends left in this administration. I need you now, Gwen needs you. I do not have time for the endless press innuendo based on jealousy that seems to pass for news in this country. I want you to be part of the success of this project.

LAWRENCE: I understand, sir.

ARTHUR: Good, then we can move forward.

MORGAN enters.

MORGAN: There has been a vote.

LAWRENCE: You are briefing the party against us.

MORGAN: The party is not blind. It looks after itself.

ARTHUR: Am I to be allowed to address the people?

MORGAN: I thought an interview would be best.

ARTHUR: Really, with who?

MORGAN: Kelly, at the News.

LAWRENCE: You cannot allow this man to dictate to you.

ARTHUR: Please, Lawrence.

MORGAN: I have briefed Kelly. She will be offering you a dignified exit.

MORGAN passes ARTHUR a press release.

LAWRENCE: How dare you presume that the President will be resigning.

MORGAN: As his broadcast will confirm, it is in the best interests of the country.

LAWRENCE: It is for the people to decide who is President.

MORGAN: An election will be announced. We are currently organising the results.

LAWRENCE: You cannot control the will of the people.

MORGAN: Lawrence, for someone at the heart of the project it has obviously been difficult for you to look out beyond your own private concerns.

LAWRENCE: I demand you retract.

MORGAN: The News have already prepared an article on your recent activities. Do you want to read it?

MORGAN passes LAWRENCE a printed sheet.

LAWRENCE: You will not be able to substantiate these rumours.

MORGAN: Really. I rather think we will.

ARTHUR: Lawrence, please.

MORGAN: There is no need for you to resign, Lawrence. You will not form part of the next administration

MORGAN (*moves to the podium and begins his speech*): It is my privilege today to pay tribute. Arthur has been a fine leader both for the party and, more importantly, for the country. He has provided wise counsel and firm leadership in times of domestic and international concern. It has taken a great toll on him personally. There is less room for principles in the real world of real politik. It is these principles that he has strived maintain that have become the greatest casualty of the last few months. We have witnessed a sense of drift as the wolves have closed upon us and it is now more than ever that we need clear thought and leadership. It is because of this that I have decided at this time to put my name forward...

Morgan's image is on screen. Then 'instructions', 'the leadership election', 'vote now'. GWEN and LAWRENCE enter.

GWEN: Did you see the broadcast?

LAWRENCE: Yes... it was quite a performance.

GWEN: The power of the people.

LAWRENCE: The world has changed and we have not even noticed.

GWEN: Morgan always wanted to be leader.

LAWRENCE: I did not understand your world.

GWEN: No, but you believed in it.

LAWRENCE: Then I was a fool.

GWEN: No, you had principles.

LAWRENCE: I didn't stick to them.

GWEN: No one does.

LAWRENCE: I think Arthur did.

GWEN: What of us, Lawrence?

LAWRENCE: We were part of our own imagination, Gwen. There is nothing for us now.

GWEN: I believe that you still love me.

LAWRENCE: Of course I do, but I don't know where that will lead us. I say 'I love you' – what does that mean? How can I make that love to be of use to us?

GWEN: Love doesn't need to be of any use.

LAWRENCE: It needs to be practical.

GWEN: Then we have done all this for nothing.

LAWRENCE: It was not nothing. We have loved each other. It has been important for me. I can see things in a way that is new.

GWEN: Then leave with me?

LAWRENCE: The press will follow us.

GWEN: They will get bored of the story. There will always be scandals to divert them.

LAWRENCE: I can't.

GWEN: No, perhaps not. Time for me to do something useful. I will not forget you Lawrence, you have become part of my life.

LAWRENCE leaves. GWEN is deciding what to pack and looks at photographs, books, etc. ARTHUR enters.

ARTHUR: Have you been packing?

GWEN: No, not yet. Just looking at our things. We used to travel so lightly.

ARTHUR: We collect as we go through.

GWEN: I'm trying to decide what I need.

ARTHUR: Anything I can help with?

GWEN: No, I don't think so.

ARTHUR: Very well...

GWEN: Arthur...

ARTHUR: Yes?

GWEN: I'm sorry about all of this.

ARTHUR: I know.

GWEN: It's just got out of hand. We're different people. I didn't want it to end like this.

ARTHUR: Sometimes events, people, they are beyond our control.

GWEN: I wanted to be part of our life, Arthur, I really did.

ARTHUR: Gwen, there is no need to blame yourself. We are all part of this world. I am human. I wish it hadn't happened this way too. But it has. We had good intentions, they just got lost on the way.

GWEN: But what of the future, now?

ARTHUR: I will go on. I am still the President.

GWEN: I thought you were resigning?

ARTHUR: I have reconsidered. The broadcast has been edited. Morgan has over-reached himself. He does not have the power within the party that everyone feared.

GWEN: You will stand against him?

ARTHUR: Morgan will not be allowed to stand. After all the people love me, remember?

GWEN: The people think you are a good deal.

ARTHUR: Then I will not disappoint them. I haven't come this far to be forgotten. I will go on. Politics, like love, is a battle. And in that, all is fair.

GWEN leaves. ARTHUR stands at the podium and waits.

ARTHUR: I am here today – as someone who has learned. The truth is before you – I can do nothing about it – it has happened – I bear no malice towards the people who I have loved... I have heard the threats from within – time has caught us – and also from you, the media, the people – I am Arthur – your leader – you expect certain qualities of such a man. It's easy just to give up – walk away. I have learned that I am not that type of man.

The watching, shadowy figure of MORGAN is projected on screen. ARTHUR turns to face it, as the lights fade.

Alison John and Ceris Jones

photograph by Simon Gough

Biographies

Greg Cullen

Greg Cullen has worked as an actor, director and writer with the East End Theatre Group; Harlow Theatre Van; Chats Palace Community Arts Centre, Hackney; and The Grove Theatre, Hammersmith.

In 1983 he moved to Wales as Writer in Residence at Theatr Powys and for twelve years was writer and artistic director for Mid-Powys Youth Theatre. He has written for radio, film and television as well as for theatre and his work has won several awards. *Past Caring* (1984) was featured by ASSITEJ as an outstanding play for young audiences; *Taken Out* (1985) was part of a season of new radio plays to win a Sony Award; and *Mary Morgan* (1988) won the City Limits Award for New Expressionism.

In 1989 *Frida and Diego* won the Fringe First Award at the Edinburgh Festival and was selected in 1994 for the BT National Connections Festival.

In 1996 *Birdbrain* was winner of the Wales Film Council/BBC Competition for a Short Film to celebrate a hundred years of cinema.

Amongst his numerous large-cast stage plays are *Tarzanne* (1988), *An Informer's Duty* (1991-2), *The Ark* (1992), *Little Devils* (1994), *Ice Cream* (2003), *Whispers in the Woods* (2004). A new touring production of *Paul Robeson Knew My Father* (2004). Amongst his adaptations are *Hard Times* (1980), *The Snow Queen* (1986), *Lysistrata* (1992) and *Silas Marner* (1996). His publications include *Greg Cullen: Three Plays* (Seren, 1998) and 'The Graveyard of Ambition?' in Anna-Marie Taylor's (ed.) *Staging Wales* (University of Wales Press, 1997).

He has worked for several theatre companies, the WNO, the Royal Welsh College of Music and Drama and the University of Wales, Aberystwyth. He is currently Director of the National Youth Theatre of Wales.

Lewis Davies

Lewis Davies is a novelist, short-story writer, publisher and playwright.

Amongst his plays are *Without Leave* (1998), *My Piece of Happiness* (1998), *Sex and Power at the Beau Rivage* (2003) and *Football* (2004).

His travel book *Freeways, A Journey West on Route 66* won the 1994 John Morgan Award and in 1999 he won the Rhys Davies Prize for *Mr Rooprantna's Chocolate*.

His novels include *Work, Sex and Rugby* (1993), *Tree of Crows* (1996), and *My Piece of Happiness* (2000).

As I was a Boy Fishing – a collection of essays, vignettes and poems – was published in 2003.

Sharon Morgan

Sharon Morgan was born in Carmarthenshire and educated at The Queen Elizabeth Grammar School for Girls, Carmarthen. She graduated in History at the University of Wales, Cardiff. Beginning an acting career in 1970 with Theatr Cymru, she has since worked extensively in theatre, film, television and radio.

In 1998 she won a BAFTA award for her performance as Mary Murphy in *Tair Chwaer (Three Sisters)* – a Gaucho production for S4C.

She has translated and adapted Simone de Beauvoir's *Monologue* as *Desperate Hopes and Fragile Dreams* and played the role of Muriel in Theatr y Byd's tour. The first version of *Magic Threads* was read at the 1996 National Eisteddfod in Welsh, entitled *Ede Hud*.

Sharon Morgan has written for Radio Cymru's *Ponty* and for S4C's *Y Palmant Aur*. Her full-length play *Dreaming Amelia* (Hi-Jinx) toured England and Wales in 2002. She has translated the *Vagina Monologues* into Welsh as *Shinanin Siarad* (Rhosys Cochion).

Chris Morgan — Director

Chris was born in Cardiff and trained at the Royal Welsh College of Music and Drama.

He has been the Associate Director of Hijinx since 2001, directing *Dreaming Amelia, I Shot Buffalo Bill* and *Paul Robeson Knew My Father* for the company.

For Theatr y Byd he directed *Inside Out – A Portrait of Ivor Novello, Sex and Power at the Beau Rivage* and *Flowers from Tunisia.*

He has also directed at the Redgrave Theatre, Farnham and the Royal Welsh College of Music and Drama.

Hijinx Theatre

Hijinx Theatre have made a steady contribution to the new writing scene in Wales for the past twenty or so years and this book confirms their ongoing commitment to text-based community theatre.

For those who think 'community theatre' lacks quality – because it often takes place in non-theatre venues – think again. Look at the plays – not only in this book but at the years of work – which have given so much to so many people, young and not so young, a great number of whom would not be regular theatre-goers.

My first introduction to the company was on a play humbly titled *The Fall of the Roman Empire*. Besides myself, there were four actors, a designer, director and musician working on a scenario for up to six weeks. This development period has become the cornerstone of Hijinx's success. In the world of finance everyone understands the meaning of investment but the moment it's transferred to developing an art form, we somehow become wastrels with our heads in the clouds. This is not true, as Hijinx have proved by consistently spinning this 'dream time' into theatrical gold. This development process presses the writer to think spatially from the start, the actors are on hand to test out ideas and are a central part of the creative process. The writer cannot escape the very practical nature of theatre and this is reflected in the three plays in this book, all of which have written inside their texts the form which will best tell the story.

The spaces in which Hijinx presents its work are usually small but the themes of the plays have consistently been big, as in Greg Cullen's *Paul Robeson Knew My Father*, which even in it's title contains the epic and the personal. This particular trait of telling mythic stories that can cross boundaries, of age, class, sex and race, has been a key component of Hijinx's work over the years. The timeless tale is always contemporary. It is the storyteller's art, in the form of drama, that makes this possible. Stories are much more important to us than we think, we tend to take them for granted and yet, 'We find we have named many of the most conspicuous heavenly bodies – Venus, Mars, Jupiter, Orion, Andromeda – after characters from stories.' (Christopher Booker – *The Seven Basic Plots*).

Hijinx Theatre has played a crucial part in my development as a dramatic storyteller, with plays such as, *Ill Met by Moonlight*, and *In the Bleak Midwinter*. In the creation of these works I was able to find 'my own voice' within the positive constraints of the small-scale theatre. These constraints have never meant the exclusion of music, movement, or even spectacle. Indeed Sharon Morgan's *Dreaming Amelia* tells its story using poetry and dance.

Hijinx has been known over the years for plays with songs and musical theatre in general, in a tradition that links musical hall, Bertolt Brecht and, of course, Shakespeare. In this regard, Hijinx have always had the common touch – striving for high standards does not mean the creation of an exclusive art form. It is interesting now to see Hijinx producing *Spinning the Round Table* by Lewis Davies, a play that strives consciously for the contemporary in both form and content – but which, as the title again suggests, has a mythic, eternal quality, as the characters struggle in archetypal fashion, for political power, risking all in their endeavours.

I look forward – not only to the publication of this book and the possibility of it aiding future productions of the plays included – but also to the new Hijinx stories, which are, of course, the old ones reborn in a manner that suits the age.

Charles Way
July 2005

Friends!

Why not join our Friends Scheme?

Become a Friend today and support the work of Hijinx Theatre.

Your donation and support will directly contribute to the future development of Hijinx.

As a Friend you will receive the following benefits:

>complimentary tickets to our Special Performances in Cardiff, with the opportunity to meet the cast;

>Hijinx Theatre's twice yearly newsletter, *Hi-Flyer*;

>tour schedules and publicity information.

Membership of the Friends Scheme costs £15 (individual) or £25 (couple). Please send a cheque (payable to 'Hijinx Theatre') and your contact details to:

>Hijinx Theatre
>Wales Millennium Centre
>Cardiff Bay
>Wales
>CF10 5AL
>UK.

THANK YOU

diverse probing

profound

urban

epic

comic

rural savage

new

writing

Independent
Presses
Management

www.inpressbooks.co.uk

Llyfrau ar-lein
Books on-line